The Leader You're Not...

The Leader You're Not...

and Why It's Just as Important as the Leader You Are

Scott Borba

ConnectEDD Publishing
Hanover, Pennsylvania

Dedication

For the glory of my Lord and Savior, Jesus Christ, whose grace, guidance, and love are the foundation of all I do.

To Janine, my loving wife, whose unwavering support, patience, and encouragement made this journey possible. You are my rock and my inspiration.

To Caleb, Madelyn, and Joshua—my greatest blessings and daily reminders of why I strive to be a better leader and person. Your love and laughter are my guiding light.

To my mom and dad—thank you for always believing in me and shaping me into the person I've become.

This book is as much yours as it is mine. Thank you all for being my foundation and my joy.

Copyright © 2025 by Scott Borba

All rights reserved. No part of this publication may be reproduced, distributed, or transmitted in any form or by any means, including photocopying, recording, or other electronic or mechanical methods, without the prior written permission of the publisher, except in the case of brief quotations embodied in critical reviews and certain other noncommercial uses permitted by copyright law. For permission requests, contact the publisher at: info@connecteddpublishing.com

This publication is available at discount pricing when purchased in quantity for educational purposes, promotions, or fundraisers. For inquiries and details, contact the publisher at: info@connecteddpublishing.com

Published by ConnectEDD Publishing LLC
Hanover, PA
www.connecteddpublishing.com

Cover Design: Kheila Casas

The Leader You're Not —1st ed. Paperback
ISBN   979-8-9918506-4-3

Praise for *The Leader You're Not*

Transformational leaders don't just talk about growth, they live it. They reflect deeply, strive relentlessly to improve, and actively seek feedback to elevate their impact. If you aspire to lead with this kind of authenticity and intention, *The Leader You're Not* is a must-read. Scott Borba skillfully blends research, insightful questions, and compelling real-world stories to guide leaders in examining their strengths, uncovering blind spots, and embracing the journey toward becoming the leader they truly are, not a version they're trying to imitate.

–Allyson Apsey | Educational leader, best-selling author of *Leading the Whole Teacher*, and keynote speaker

The Leader You're Not is my favorite book of the year written about school leadership. Scott Borba gets it, and this is the book for you! You're going to laugh, learn, connect, reflect, and just become a better leader. Every story and lesson from Scott is something that you can do as well in your own leadership, right away, without extra training or PD, it's all just doable. If you're ready to grow your leadership and be better for everyone you work with, *The Leader You're Not* is the book for you.

–Adam Welcome | Educator, Author, Speaker, Podcaster

No matter your current role or level of experience, this book invites you to pause and reflect on the often-unspoken realities of leadership—the gaps, the blind spots, and the parts we hope no one sees. With honesty, insight, and practical tools, it challenges you to confront what's hidden and grow from it. This is more than a leadership book—it's a call to evolve into the most authentic and impactful version of yourself.

–Jessica Gomez | Director of Continuous Improvement and Accountability, Menifee Union School District

As a school leader, I've often felt pressured to have it all together. In *The Leader You're Not*, Scott Borba offers a powerful reminder that real leadership isn't about perfection—it's about self-awareness, humility, and growth. This book offers readers permission to pause, reflect, and lead more authentically. It's a must-read for anyone who wants to lead with courage and compassion.

    –Jessica Cabeen | Principal, Speaker, Coach, Author

This is the book I wish I had when I first stepped into leadership. Scott Borba masterfully unpacks the lessons we never learned in principal school, those that truly define our ability to lead effectively. Through a pragmatic and thoughtful approach, he challenges us to embrace the leader we aren't, rather than the one we imagine ourselves to be. By recognizing our blind spots, we gain the clarity needed to lead with authenticity, humility, and impact. This book is an essential resource for any school leader committed to personal growth and lasting change.

    –Nathaniel Provencio | National School Leadership Coach

Reading *The Leader You're Not…and Why It's Just as Important as the Leader You Are* feels like having a conversation with a trusted friend and seasoned leader who isn't afraid to share his own missteps. Scott Borba brings a fresh perspective on the idea of never "arriving," embracing the continuous journey of self-awareness and growth, even in the face of adversity. By focusing on the whole principal—including imperfections—he reminds us that we are enough as we are, but that we must continuously summon the courage to risk forward and create meaningful change for the communities and students we serve. Leaders will feel seen, inspired, and empowered to grow in their own leadership journey.

    –Carmen Maring | Principal of Gull Lake Middle School

As a person who has a compelling interest in developing leadership skills in myself and others, this book was as practical and relatable as any of the many leadership books I have studied. I like how Scott Borba describes *Humble Confidence* as the balancing of strength and vulnerability, as well as his encouragement to listen more and speak less. New leaders so often fall into the trap of thinking they need to know everything, and they end up walling themselves off from important ideas and insights of others. I'm inspired by Scott's invitation to look for blind spots and approach them with curiosity as we become self-aware leaders who "dare to explore blind spots" on the way to growth, humility, and more honest connection with our team. This book is a collection of excellent learning tools, including thought-provoking questions, relatable stories, and self-assessments. I highly recommend *The Leader You're Not* to aspiring, novice, or seasoned leaders looking not only to improve, but to find more joy in leadership.

  –J. Lynn Jones | Master Trainer at *Crucial Learning*, Former School and District Administrator

A powerful invitation to lead with honesty, humility, and heart. *The Leader You're Not* redefines what it means to be effective by showing that the path to real growth begins where perfection ends. This book is a must-read for leaders ready to embrace their fully flawed selves.

  –Joy M Kelly, Ed.S. | Senior Associate, JCasas and Associates

The Leader You're Not is an inspiring call to lead with honesty, humility, and heart. It challenges leaders to embrace their blind spots, let go of perfectionism, and grow through vulnerability and feedback. With wisdom and warmth, it shows that true leadership isn't about having all the answers—it's about creating space for growth, trust, and transformation. A must-read for anyone ready to lead with purpose and authenticity!

  –Dr. Andy Jacks | Nationally Distinguished Principal and NAESP Senior Fellow

The Leader You're Not is a refreshing and courageous exploration of leadership through the lens of self-awareness, vulnerability, and personal growth. Instead of glorifying the typical hero-leader archetype, readers will enjoy going on a deeply personal journey…one that challenges assumptions, reveals blind spots, and encourages leaders to confront the aspects of themselves they often avoid.

–Jose Gonzalez | Superintendent, Planada Elementary School District

I have read many educational leadership books—this one is different! It is especially good for those just beginning their journeys in school administration. Scott provides a voice for all the feelings we experience. It's a reflective framework with real world examples of how to make the small improvements that will help the reader become the leader they always wanted to be.

–Alan Peterson | Superintendent, Merced Union High School District

The Leader You're Not arrives at the right time for school administrators who micromanage and consequently, become overwhelmed with the responsibilities and duties of the job. The book is a recipe for improving school administrator effectiveness by shifting leadership thinking. This renewed leadership mindset mitigates the burdens of school administration by "responding and adapting to personal weaknesses", not to mention, capitalizing on strengths. The outcomes further enhance trust in teachers, staff, and parents and empowers them to become shared-decision makers in the school community, with the improved prospect of experiencing higher levels of student achievement.

–John Borba, Ed.D. | Professor Emeritus California State University, Stanislaus

In *The Leader You're Not*, the author flips the leadership conversation on its head, exploring the blind spots, limitations, and unseen influences that shape every leader. With rare honesty and depth, this book invites readers to embrace what they don't know, can't do, or were never meant to be—and shows how that humility can become a powerful asset. It's a refreshing take and provides guidance for growth through reflections and examples. Great for individuals or collaborative study.

–Angel J. Barrett Ed.D. | 2009 NAESP Principal of the Year, Retired Administrator, Los Angeles Unified School District

For those ready to break old patterns and embrace actionable steps toward thoughtful, servant leadership in schools, this excellent book serves as your blueprint for *real*, meaningful change.

–John Wendel | Teacher-Leader

Today's educational leaders have the continued task of maneuvering through ongoing challenges. The author, Scott Borba, is a successful school leader whom I have had an opportunity to listen to and learn from. *The Leader You're Not…and Why It's Just as Important as the Leader You Are* is an invaluable resource for striving educational leaders to balance a unique set of skills and qualities to navigate today's challenges in education.

–Dave Steckler | Principal of Red Trail Elementary

The Leader You're Not is an inspiring and practical guide that redefines leadership in a refreshing and empowering way by encouraging leaders to embrace their true selves and leverage their strengths, offering a roadmap for authentic and impactful leadership. It emphasizes empathy, adaptability, and purpose-driven actions making this book a valuable resource for both aspiring and experienced leaders. Its engaging style and actionable advice leave readers feeling motivated and ready to enhance their leadership journey. A must-read for anyone looking to lead with integrity and purpose.

    –Bryan Ballenger Ed.D. | Superintendent, Gustine Unified School District

Borba masterfully captures the essence of what makes a truly impactful leader—not just the strengths we bring to the table, but the self-awareness to recognize where we fall short and the courage to grow from it. This book is a must-read for anyone who wants to lead with integrity, self-reflection, and a true heart for others.

    –Maria Smith | Vice-Principal of Le Grand Elementary

Table of Contents

Introduction *The Journey of Self Discovery*........................ 1

Chapter One *Beyond the Spotlight: Embracing Your Blind Spots* 7
Understanding areas of weakness you may not see and the impact they have on your leadership.

Chapter Two *Humble Confidence: Balancing Strength and Vulnerability* 17
The power of leading with humility and knowing when to show vulnerability to gain trust.

Chapter Three *The Cost of Perfectionism: Why Leaders Need to Let Go* 27
Exploring the hidden costs of striving for perfection and how it can stifle growth and morale.

Chapter Four *Listening to Criticism: Turning Weaknesses into Growth Opportunities* 37
Approaching feedback as a gift and learning from the hard truths others share.

Chapter Five *Delegate, Don't Dominate: Recognizing When to Step Back*... 49
The importance of knowing your limits and the art of empowering others.

Chapter Six *Managing Emotions: Keeping Cool Under Pressure* 63
Strategies for emotional regulation and modeling calmness in challenging situations.

Chapter Seven *The Silent Saboteurs: Addressing Insecurity and Self-Doubt* 81
How internal doubts can undermine leadership and ways to confront them.

Chapter Eight *Visible Leadership: Leading Authentically in the Face of Adversity*... 97
Embracing honesty about limitations to create a culture of trust and openness.

Chapter Nine *Adapt or Falter: When Your Leadership Style Needs to Change* 111
Knowing when and how to adjust your leadership approach to meet changing needs.

Chapter Ten *The Courage to Say No: Setting Boundaries in Leadership*... 127
The importance of setting boundaries, avoiding burnout, and aligning decisions with your goals.

TABLE OF CONTENTS

Chapter Eleven *The Role of Emotional Agility: Navigating Complexity with Grace* 141
Understanding the difference between emotional intelligence and emotional agility.

Chapter Twelve *The Art of Asking the Right Questions: Unlocking Growth Through Inquiry* 155
How thoughtful inquiry can spark creativity, encourage ownership, and drive growth.

Chapter Thirteen *Beyond Self-Awareness: Cultivating Organizational Awareness.* 167
Identifying and addressing organizational blind spots and cultural challenges.

Chapter Fourteen *The Legacy of a Self-Aware Leader: Building a Culture of Continuous Improvement* 177
How leaders who are aware of their own limitations inspire a culture of continuous improvement.

Final Thoughts *The Path of the Self-Aware Leader* 187

Recommended Reading 195

About the Author 199

More from ConnectEDD Publishing. 201

INTRODUCTION

The Journey of Self Discovery

Leadership is hard to define, yet unmistakable when witnessed. We recognize it in moments of inspiration, when someone rallies us to reach higher, think bigger, or care more deeply. But ask anyone who has stood at the helm of a school, business, or community initiative, and they'll tell you that leadership is far more than its celebrated moments. Real leadership often hides in the quiet, unnoticed actions, the uncelebrated decisions, and the honest self-reflection on mistakes made along the way.

This book is about the unspoken side of leadership, about what goes unseen—the gaps and flaws we often choose to ignore, hoping no one else will notice. As public school leaders, we're typically trained to focus on our strengths and project confidence and competence. Yet, as you'll see, true leadership strength is not achieved by denying weaknesses but by understanding and embracing them. Paradoxically, the weaknesses we hide may hold the key to the greatest influence we can have.

You might be here because you've been feeling stretched too thin, navigating a stream of challenges that no amount of training seemed to cover. Or maybe you feel an unrelenting need to meet the standards set by those around you—teachers, parents, students, other leaders—who look to you for answers, direction, and hope. Maybe there's a quiet part of you that wonders if you're enough. And if that's the case, you're in the right place.

There's a trap that catches many leaders, particularly in education, and it's the myth of the "complete leader." This mythical leader is sharp-minded, adaptable, and endlessly resourceful, who is equally comfortable leading an all-staff meeting as resolving an unexpected parent crisis. It's someone who appears unflappable and all-knowing. This myth sets us up for failure because, in truth, no leader can embody every quality needed for every situation. The beauty—and the challenge—of leadership lies in our capacity to grow, to learn, and to draw on strengths and weaknesses alike.

If this book does one thing, I hope it lifts the weight of perfectionism from your shoulders. As you read, you'll come to see that embracing what you are not is *not* a weakness. It is, in fact, a profound act of courage and humility. You'll discover that authentic leadership involves taking stock of your vulnerabilities, recognizing your blind spots, and turning these into learning opportunities. As public school leaders, we're in the business of building up others. But if we're honest, our ability to do so depends on our commitment to building up ourselves—not through sheer self-confidence, but through self-awareness and the pursuit of growth.

Why the Leader You're Not Matters

Leaders have long been praised for their unique strengths. You'll read articles about cultivating resilience, learning to "grit" through adversity, or developing charisma. Yet, rarely are we called to look directly at our flaws, our biases, our own insecurities. In a field like education, where stakes are high and lives are profoundly impacted, we must consider what is missing from this narrative. For example, if we lack patience, we may unintentionally cut off learning opportunities for the more reserved voices on our team. If we fear conflict, we might delay important, constructive conversations, hoping issues resolve themselves.

It may seem counterintuitive to give as much attention to the aspects of leadership we struggle with as to those in which we excel. But to be an effective leader, you must understand how to handle the "negative" side of the leadership equation. Consider this: a teacher isn't an effective role model simply because they know their subject matter inside and out. They also need empathy to understand their students, patience to repeat explanations, and humility to admit when they don't know an answer. Likewise, as leaders, we're more than a list of qualities; we're a complex mix of traits, motivations, fears, and ambitions. By exploring our limitations as well as our strengths, we broaden our range, strengthening our ability to lead authentically and effectively.

How Ignoring Weaknesses Undermines Leadership

It's tempting to ignore or sidestep our weaknesses, particularly when they feel like cracks in the facade of a capable leader. Society and organizational culture often suggest that good leaders are those who charge forward with assurance, who keep their heads up and their doubts out of view. But the truth is, overlooking your weaknesses doesn't make you stronger; it limits your ability to respond and adapt. Imagine a teacher who refuses to acknowledge they struggle with organization. That gap will inevitably show up—whether in rushed lesson plans, missed deadlines, or an overwhelmed sense of trying to stay afloat. For leaders, these unacknowledged areas create stress, hamper productivity, and erode trust over time.

As we explore these ideas together, I invite you to shift your perspective on what leadership means. What if we allowed for moments where we didn't have all the answers, where our vulnerability became a source of connection rather than a cause for shame? What if our teams and schools saw us not as infallible figures, but as resilient, learning leaders who model growth and self-awareness? This book will argue that owning your limitations isn't just beneficial—it's essential. The leader who refuses to examine their weaknesses inevitably risks being limited by them. Conversely, the leader who embraces what they're not gains the freedom to grow and evolve beyond any preconceived role.

A Journey into Honest Self-Reflection

Throughout this book, we'll explore many aspects of leadership through the lens of what you are *not*. Each chapter will invite you to examine the dimensions of leadership that are often overlooked. Together, we'll look at the real-world implications of perfectionism, the impact of emotional transparency, and the need for genuine and productive delegation. We'll talk about things like imposter syndrome, handling conflict, and adapting to change—not in an abstract sense, but in the context of your day-to-day leadership in public schools. And while the examples here speak specifically to educators and school administrators, these concepts apply universally to leaders in any field.

This journey will ask you to confront parts of yourself that may feel uncomfortable. You'll look at the things you wish you were better at, the moments you've stumbled, and the areas you've avoided out of fear. But take heart: as you face these areas with honesty and courage, you'll uncover new strengths and a renewed sense of purpose. You may even find that the qualities you once viewed as weaknesses can serve as unexpected assets, allowing you to approach your work with greater empathy and perspective.

Reframing the Leadership Mindset

Ultimately, "The Leader You're Not" is about redefining leadership. It's about moving beyond titles, accolades, and the external markers of success to focus on the internal journey of self-discovery. When we acknowledge our weaknesses, we open the door to real, transformative growth—not only for ourselves but for those we lead. As you engage with this material, keep in mind that growth is an ongoing process. True leadership isn't about perfection; it's about a willingness to reflect, to change, and to grow.

So, as you turn the page, I encourage you to leave behind any preconceived notions of what a leader should be. Instead, let's explore together what it means to be a leader who knows themselves fully, who recognizes the importance of both strengths and limitations, and who strives to grow—not despite their weaknesses but because of them. Here's to the leader you are, *and* the leader you're not.

LESSONS LEARNED

At the end of each chapter, you'll find a "Lessons Learned" story—an illustrative example that brings the chapter's ideas to life. While the names of the leaders, schools, and districts you'll encounter are fictional, these stories are not purely imaginary. Each scenario is drawn from the lived experiences of real school leaders, condensed and adapted to protect anonymity and ensure readability. By presenting these composites, I hope to show how the principles discussed in each chapter can be applied in actual educational settings. Think of these stories not as distant case studies, but as practical, relatable narratives—proving that the concepts explored here are not just ideals, but workable strategies that have helped leaders guide their communities toward positive change.

CHAPTER ONE

Beyond the Spotlight: Embracing Your Blind Spots

Let's begin with a story. Picture a school principal named Michael, a man who wakes up each morning with the distinct feeling that he has to "bring his best self." On any given day, you'll find him meticulously dressed, hair neat, tie perfectly knotted, each step forward an attempt to embody the role of "the leader." In the halls, he greets students and teachers with the same warm, controlled enthusiasm he believes they expect from him. But Michael has a secret, one he probably doesn't even fully realize himself.

You see, Michael is terrified of not being enough. He never hesitates to jump into a problem, striving to resolve issues the second they arise, always proving himself useful. But his eagerness has a price. What Michael doesn't see—what he's blind to—is how his quick-fix approach inadvertently undercuts the autonomy of his teachers. His staff feels stifled, unable to take initiative or think creatively, all because Michael's well-intentioned interventions have created a kind of dependency. The school hums with a quiet tension that Michael himself doesn't understand, let alone notice.

This story is not unique to Michael. It's a universal reality: as leaders, we all have blind spots—parts of our behavior, attitudes, or ways of operating that we can't see but that everyone around us feels. In fact, many leaders have learned that they are often the last to realize the impact of their own behavior. We're so focused on what we think is necessary for "strong leadership" that we miss the unintended ripple effects of our actions.

This chapter is about uncovering those blind spots and stepping away from the comfort zone of what we know—or think we know—about ourselves. We're going to get uncomfortable, perhaps even a little embarrassed, because to fully understand our impact on others, we need to look honestly at ourselves. But by doing so, we'll gain valuable insights that allow us to become better leaders, more in tune with our teams and, ultimately, more effective.

The Anatomy of a Blind Spot

Blind spots, by nature, are things we can't see. They're the traits, habits, and assumptions that feel natural or right to us but which might be unintentionally harmful. We all have them, no matter how self-aware we believe ourselves to be. And yet, addressing them can be one of the most challenging components of leadership.

In Michael's case, his blind spot was his need to always be the "problem solver." He was so fixated on appearing competent and engaged that he missed how his presence created a dependency on him to solve every issue. He genuinely believed he was doing the right thing. And that's the tricky part: blind spots often masquerade as strengths, or at least as harmless habits.

But here's the reality—left unchecked, blind spots will derail us, causing frustration for our teams and, over time, eroding trust. This isn't about fixing every flaw but about being open enough to recognize where our behaviors may be working against our intentions.

Strategies for Discovering Your Blind Spots

Identifying your blind spots is a process, one that requires humility, openness, and a willingness to lean into discomfort. Here are several practical ways to uncover these hidden areas and begin addressing them constructively:

1. **Ask for Honest Feedback—And Listen**

The most direct way to discover blind spots is to ask the people you lead. This may seem obvious, but genuine, constructive feedback is hard to come by if you're not intentional about seeking it. The key is not just to ask but to ask in a way that signals you're open to hearing the truth, no matter how uncomfortable it might be.

Consider scheduling a regular "feedback day," when you invite team members to share their thoughts on your leadership style. A few pointers for creating a feedback-friendly environment:

Ask open-ended questions: Instead of "How am I doing?" try "What's one thing I do that could be holding our team back?" or "Can you describe a time when I may have unintentionally made things harder for you?"

Be consistent: One feedback session won't give you the full picture. Make this a regular practice to build trust and signal that you genuinely value their input.

Listen without defending: Resist the urge to explain or justify your actions. Just absorb the information, take notes, and thank them for their honesty. Reflect on the feedback and revisit it later when you're alone, to see what resonates.

2. **Notice Patterns in Interactions**

Blind spots often become evident when we pay attention to recurring patterns in our relationships or situations. If you find that the same kinds of conflicts or misunderstandings arise repeatedly, this could be a clue to an underlying blind spot. Try keeping a "leadership journal" for a month, noting situations where you felt resistance or frustration from others. Ask yourself:

"Is there a common theme in the feedback I receive?"

"Are there patterns in the way others respond to me during challenging conversations?"

"What do I tend to assume about people or situations without questioning?"

This kind of self-observation can be a powerful way to see yourself from an outsider's perspective.

3. **Invite 360-Degree Reviews**

A 360-degree review allows you to receive feedback not only from your direct reports but also from peers, supervisors, and even community members if relevant. This method is often more anonymous, which can encourage greater honesty.

When you receive your 360-degree feedback, look for areas where multiple people noted similar observations. If three people mention that you often interrupt during discussions, there's a good chance this is a behavior worth examining. Don't get defensive about feedback that surprises you. Instead, view it as an opportunity to uncover something you might not otherwise see.

4. **Reflect on Emotional Responses**

Our emotional responses to situations often hold clues to our blind spots. For example, if you feel defensive or irritated when someone gives you feedback, ask yourself why. Are you reacting because the feedback hit a nerve, perhaps revealing something you didn't want to admit?

Keep track of these emotional responses in your journal. Note situations where you felt strong negative emotions and examine whether they could be related to a blind spot. For instance, if you find yourself reacting poorly to suggestions, it could indicate that you have a blind spot around control or collaboration.

5. **Work with a Leadership Coach or Mentor**
    Sometimes it takes an outside perspective to see what's hidden in plain sight. A leadership coach or mentor can offer constructive, unbiased feedback and help you work through blind spots. Coaches, in particular, are trained to listen and ask the kinds of questions that bring underlying issues to light.

    If a formal coach isn't available, consider asking a trusted colleague or peer to provide this insight. Explain that you're working on becoming more self-aware and ask them to point out any patterns or behaviors they've noticed. The key here is choosing someone you respect who can provide honest feedback without fear of damaging the relationship.

Turning Blind Spots into Strengths

Once you've identified some of your blind spots, the question becomes: what now? Awareness alone isn't enough to effect change; we need to turn these insights into strengths.

1. **Practice Self-Awareness Through Mindfulness**
    Mindfulness isn't just a buzzword; it's a skill that helps us slow down and observe our own thoughts, feelings, and actions without judgment. For leaders, mindfulness can be transformative. It allows you to become more aware of your habits and behaviors in real time, which can help you avoid automatically falling into old patterns.

    Consider starting a daily mindfulness practice, even if it's just a few minutes a day. This can be as simple as taking five minutes each

morning to sit quietly and observe your thoughts. Over time, this practice will help you recognize your behaviors more clearly, allowing you to act with intention rather than reflex.

2. **Use Feedback to Set Personal Goals**

Blind spots can feel daunting because they're often complex, rooted in habits formed over years. The key is to tackle them one step at a time. Start by setting small, measurable goals related to the feedback you received.

For example, if you've learned that you tend to monopolize meetings, set a goal to ask open-ended questions during each team discussion or to pause and give others a chance to speak before offering your own thoughts. Over time, these small adjustments will lead to noticeable change.

3. **Develop a "Growth Mindset" Around Weaknesses**

One of the biggest obstacles in addressing blind spots is the belief that they reflect fundamental flaws. But the truth is, these areas of weakness are often areas of potential growth. Adopting a growth mindset—the idea that our skills and abilities can be developed—can make all the difference. When you view blind spots as areas to improve rather than immutable traits, they become less intimidating and more actionable.

4. **Regularly Revisit and Reflect**

Blind spots are not things you identify once and move on from. They can evolve, change, and show up in new forms over time. Make a habit of revisiting your personal feedback, checking in on progress, and seeking new insights from others. This will allow you to continually fine-tune your self-awareness and prevent blind spots from catching you off guard.

Conclusion

One of the greatest acts of courage on any leadership journey is to look at ourselves in the mirror without flinching. Identifying and acknowledging our blind spots is not a quick fix; it's a commitment to lifelong growth and awareness. As you begin to uncover the areas you hadn't noticed before, remember that the goal isn't to achieve some flawless version of yourself, nor is it to get every part of leadership "right." Rather, it's about recognizing where there's room to evolve and leaning into that space with honesty and humility.

Leaders who acknowledge their blind spots earn something far more valuable than an image of perfection—they gain the trust and respect of those around them. When you show others that you're willing to be vulnerable, to grow, and to learn, you create a ripple effect. This willingness to confront your own limitations fosters a culture of openness, a place where others feel safe doing the same. And in an educational setting, where trust and integrity are everything, that level of authenticity can transform your school or team into a community where everyone feels empowered to bring their best selves, imperfections and all.

> This willingness to confront your own limitations fosters a culture of openness, a place where others feel safe doing the same.

With an initial understanding of your blind spots, you're laying the foundation for deeper self-awareness. But awareness alone doesn't make you an effective leader. Next, we're going to explore a quality that helps leaders strike a powerful balance: humble confidence. This paradoxical combination allows you to lead with strength while embracing vulnerability. It's about being grounded enough to trust your abilities without needing to prove yourself at every turn and courageous enough to admit when you're uncertain.

In Chapter Two, we'll delve into what humble confidence looks like in practice. We'll look at how to hold space for others' ideas, even when you feel the pressure to have all the answers. We'll talk about how true humility can actually enhance your authority, inviting your team to share in your vision while still recognizing your role as their guide. This balance of humility and confidence is essential for leaders who want to build authentic, lasting influence—and it's what will ultimately set you apart as a leader who inspires not by perfection, but by example.

So as you step beyond the spotlight of certainty and ego, let's journey toward the heart of leadership: not by projecting an image of flawless competence, but by cultivating a confidence that's firmly rooted in self-acceptance and open to growth.

Self-Reflection Prompt

As you close this chapter, take a moment to consider your own leadership journey. Reflect on the roles you play, the responsibilities you carry, and how you think others perceive you. Awareness of our blind spots starts with asking the right questions and being honest with ourselves.

Reflection Question

Think back to a recent interaction with your team, staff, or students. Is there a chance that your actions or words might have impacted others in unintended ways? If so, what assumptions might have been driving your behavior, and how could you approach similar situations differently in the future to foster more collaboration, autonomy, or understanding? Take some time to write your reflections, even if they feel incomplete. These insights can be powerful tools as you continue to grow in your self-awareness and leadership.

LESSONS LEARNED

Nicole was a first-year principal who believed her enthusiasm and hands-on approach were key strengths. She was everywhere—popping into classrooms unannounced, sending lengthy, detail-rich emails to staff about new ideas, and stepping into lessons to model teaching strategies. She saw herself as supportive, but over time, something felt off. Several of her most trusted teachers seemed distant. Their once-warm smiles were fading, and the honest, lively discussions they'd had before she became principal had grown stilted.

Curious and increasingly concerned, Nicole decided to do something uncomfortable: invite feedback. She scheduled a series of informal coffee chats with her staff, asking them about the school climate, communication, and her leadership style. She made it clear she genuinely wanted their perspectives, even if it was hard to hear.

At first, everyone hesitated. Eventually, Ms. Gomez, a well-respected veteran teacher, gently explained that Nicole's constant classroom drop-ins felt more like supervision than support. It made teachers feel scrutinized, not trusted. Others agreed, adding that Nicole's long, directive emails made them feel micromanaged and uncertain about their own judgment. A few newer teachers mentioned they admired her energy but wished she'd step back and listen to their challenges before offering solutions.

None of this feedback was easy for Nicole to hear. She realized she'd been leaning heavily into what she perceived as her strengths—her visibility, energy, and wealth of ideas—without considering how they might be affecting others. In focusing so intently on what she did well, she'd ignored her blind spot: the team's need for trust, autonomy, and a principal who listened as much as she led.

Armed with this insight, Nicole recalibrated. She set a personal goal: whenever she walked into a classroom, she would stay at the back, observe quietly, and follow up with reflective questions instead of immediate suggestions. She shortened her emails, focusing on essentials and asking for input. More importantly, she intentionally left space for teachers to share their thoughts before offering her own ideas.

Over a few months, the atmosphere lightened. Teachers began speaking up more frequently in meetings and seemed more comfortable in conversations with Nicole. By acknowledging and embracing her blind spots—her tendency to over-insert herself and her struggle to truly listen—Nicole grew into a leader whose presence felt collaborative, not controlling.

In this way, the theory from Chapter One came to life: by recognizing her blind spots, seeking honest feedback, and making small but meaningful changes, Nicole used self-awareness to become a more effective, trusted leader.

CHAPTER TWO

Humble Confidence: Balancing Strength and Vulnerability

If there's one trait that sets apart great leaders, it's confidence—or so we're often told. But for those of us leading in schools, communities, and organizations in which every action is magnified, confidence alone isn't enough. What we need instead is a more nuanced quality: humble confidence. It's an approach that combines the strength of self-assurance with the humility to admit when we don't have all the answers. This balance between strength and vulnerability is a defining aspect of powerful, authentic leadership, and it builds the kind of trust that can transform a team or a school culture.

Humble confidence may sound contradictory, but in reality, it's the kind of mindset that allows you to lead with integrity, inspire loyalty, and empower others. So let's dive into what humble confidence looks like in practice, why it matters, and how you can cultivate it as a leader.

The Foundation of Humble Confidence

To understand humble confidence, we need to break down its two core components: humility and confidence. Humility is the willingness to acknowledge our limitations, to be teachable, and to value others' contributions. Confidence, on the other hand, is rooted in self-belief, in knowing that we bring valuable skills, experience, and insights to our role. When these two qualities merge, they create a powerful balance that allows leaders to lead with strength while remaining open, approachable, and genuinely connected to those around them.

Think of humble confidence as a balance between owning your role and authority as a leader while also creating space for others. It's about setting aside ego and welcoming collaboration, even if that means you won't always have the final word or be the hero of the story.

> **Think of humble confidence as a balance between owning your role and authority as a leader while also creating space for others.**

The Power of Vulnerability in Leadership

Brené Brown, a well-known researcher on vulnerability, has shown us that vulnerability isn't weakness—in fact, it's one of the most courageous acts we can perform. When leaders are willing to show vulnerability, they demonstrate authenticity. This authenticity creates trust because people can see that you are a real person, just like them. This doesn't mean oversharing personal struggles or doubting yourself in every situation; rather, it's about knowing when to acknowledge challenges, admit mistakes, or ask for help.

Here's an example: imagine you're in a staff meeting, and a complex problem arises. Instead of immediately jumping to a solution, you might say, "I don't have all the answers for this, but I know that, together, we can find a path forward." In that moment, you're demonstrating humble confidence. You're strong enough to admit your limitations but confident enough to believe in the collective power of your team.

Practical Strategies for Cultivating Humble Confidence

While humble confidence may come naturally to some, it's also a mindset and skill that can be developed. Here are several practical strategies to help you cultivate this balance in your leadership role:

1. **Recognize and Challenge Your Inner Critic**

    Every leader has an inner voice that questions their capabilities or qualifications, especially in challenging moments. This inner critic can make it difficult to show confidence, often pushing us to overcompensate with a "know-it-all" attitude or a reluctance to show vulnerability. The first step in cultivating humble confidence is to become aware of this inner critic and challenge it.

    Take a moment to reflect on times when you've felt the need to be "perfect" or when you've been afraid to show vulnerability. Ask yourself:

    What is my inner critic saying in these moments?

    What am I afraid of if I let others see my uncertainty?

    Acknowledge that everyone, even the most accomplished leaders, experiences moments of doubt. Humble confidence is about not allowing these moments to control you. Rather than listening to your inner critic, remind yourself that embracing imperfection is part of growth, both for you and for your team.

2. **Listen More, Speak Less**

    One of the simplest but most powerful ways to demonstrate humility is to listen. When you actively listen to others, you communicate respect and openness, and you signal that you don't need to dominate every conversation. Active listening also builds trust because it shows that you value your team members' insights and perspectives. In practice, this means:

- Giving team members time and space to share their ideas without immediately interjecting.
- Asking questions that encourage others to expand on their thoughts rather than offering solutions right away.
- Reflecting on what you've heard to ensure that you understand and to validate others' contributions.

For example, if a teacher comes to you with a concern about a new curriculum, you might say, "Tell me more about how this has been affecting your students." By truly listening, you demonstrate humility and create a safe space for your team to share openly. This approach fosters collaboration and opens the door for solutions that might not have emerged if you had immediately taken charge of the situation.

3. Admit When You're Wrong—And Make It Right

Admitting mistakes is one of the hardest, yet most powerful, ways to demonstrate humble confidence. It's a natural human instinct to want to appear right, especially as leaders who are often looked to for guidance. But acknowledging a mistake is a mark of strong, humble leadership.

Imagine you made a decision that unintentionally added extra work for teachers. Instead of brushing it off, acknowledge it openly: "I realize that my decision on scheduling has created additional challenges for you, and that wasn't my intention. I appreciate your patience, and I'm committed to finding a way to lighten that load." Taking accountability in this way builds credibility, shows that you're human, and reinforces the trust between you and your team.

Mistakes are inevitable, but how you handle them can either strengthen or weaken your relationships with others. Leaders who can admit their mistakes and take steps to make them right show that they care more about the team's well-being than their own ego.

> **Mistakes are inevitable, but how you handle them can either strengthen or weaken your relationships with others.**

4. Seek Input and Be Open to Feedback

One of the best ways to lead with humble confidence is to actively seek input from those you lead. Soliciting feedback not only helps you grow but also shows your team that their voices matter. It's a powerful way to model humility while building a collaborative culture. Create opportunities for feedback through:

- Regular check-ins with individual team members where you ask about their thoughts on your leadership style.
- Anonymous surveys that allow staff to provide honest feedback without fear of repercussions.
- Feedback loops, where you follow up on the feedback received and share what actions you're taking based on their input.

For instance, after implementing a new policy, you might ask, "How has this change impacted you? Is there anything you think we should adjust?" By doing this, you show confidence in your leadership, but also the humility to recognize that no decision is set in stone and that others' perspectives are invaluable.

5. **Celebrate Others' Successes—Not Just Your Own**

Humble confidence means recognizing that the success of your school or team isn't solely your doing. It's the result of a collective effort, and celebrating others' achievements shows that you value and respect everyone's contributions. Make it a habit to acknowledge and celebrate the achievements of those around you. Send an email highlighting a teacher's innovative lesson plan, publicly acknowledge the contributions of staff members in meetings, or simply give a genuine "thank you" to someone who has gone above and beyond.

When you celebrate others' successes, you show that you're confident enough not to need the spotlight for yourself. This helps create a culture of mutual respect and reinforces that everyone's contributions matter.

The Impact of Humble Confidence on School Culture

When leaders embrace humble confidence, it has a profound effect on the entire school culture. Humility in leadership makes it safe for everyone to be open, take risks, and learn from mistakes. Confidence, on the other hand, sets a standard for self-assurance and resilience, showing others that they can trust your leadership even when challenges arise.

By modeling humble confidence, you'll find that others are more willing to collaborate, share their ideas, and step up as leaders in their own right. Staff members will feel empowered to bring their full selves to work because they know they're part of a team where honesty, trust, and mutual respect are valued above ego or status.

A leader's mindset is contagious. When you approach challenges with humble confidence, your team takes notice. They see that you're willing to own your strengths but also face your weaknesses head-on, and this encourages them to do the same.

Think of humble confidence as an invitation for others to lead authentically. When teachers see their principal acknowledging mistakes, it gives them permission to take risks in their own classrooms without fear of judgment. When support staff witness you listening to feedback and adjusting your approach, they feel their own contributions are valued, strengthening their commitment to the shared mission.

Over time, this approach doesn't just build trust—it creates a resilient team that can face challenges with unity and creativity. And as a leader, you'll find that this culture of humility and strength opens doors to deeper relationships, greater innovation, and a shared commitment to continuous growth.

Conclusion: Embracing Humble Confidence as Your Leadership Foundation

Humble confidence is a cornerstone of authentic, impactful leadership. By balancing strength with humility, you create an atmosphere of trust, openness, and genuine collaboration. You show your team that leadership isn't about perfection but about commitment to growth, resilience, and collective purpose. In education, where every choice affects students, staff, and the broader community, leading with humble confidence becomes an invaluable asset. It allows you to guide your team with assurance, even as you remain receptive to feedback, new ideas, and the strengths of others.

As you continue to cultivate humble confidence, remember that it's not about being the loudest or most knowledgeable voice in the room. Rather, it's about knowing when to stand firm and when to step back, when to encourage others to lead, and when to acknowledge your own limitations. By embracing both your strengths and vulnerabilities, you're not only showing your team what authentic leadership looks like—you're giving them permission to do the same.

As leaders, it's easy to believe that if we strive for perfection, we'll be seen as credible, competent, and deserving of respect. But this pursuit often leads to exhaustion, frustration, and missed opportunities for genuine connection and growth. In the next chapter, we'll explore how perfectionism can hinder leaders and limit their teams. We'll dive into the hidden costs of aiming for flawlessness, how it impacts decision-making, creativity, and morale, and how learning to let go of perfection can lead to more authentic, effective leadership.

We'll challenge the notion of perfection as a standard and discuss practical ways to embrace progress over perfection. By releasing the need to get everything "just right," you'll free yourself to lead with greater flexibility, inspire innovation within your team, and cultivate a healthier, more sustainable approach to leadership.

Self-Reflection Prompt

As you reflect on humble confidence, think about moments in your leadership journey when you felt the tension between needing to appear strong and wanting to show vulnerability. Consider the balance you strive for between listening to others and standing firm in your decisions.

Reflection Question

Can you recall a recent time when humility or confidence alone didn't feel like enough? What happened, and how might blending humility with confidence have changed the situation? As you look back, what would you say to yourself in that moment to encourage a balanced, open approach? Write your thoughts, and keep them in mind as you practice humble confidence in the future. These reflections can guide you in finding new ways to embrace both your strengths and your openness as a leader.

LESSONS LEARNED

Jamal had been the assistant principal at Pine Grove Middle School for three years before stepping into the principal role. He prided himself on his steady calmness, policy knowledge, and ability to keep the school running smoothly. At the same time, he'd always been uneasy about one aspect of his leadership: delivering tough feedback to his staff.

At his first staff meeting as principal, Jamal stood in front of thirty teachers who were curious, hopeful, and maybe a bit wary. Pine Grove had recently implemented a new reading curriculum, and some teachers were struggling with the transition. They needed guidance and support, but Jamal knew that in a few cases, he'd have to address practices that were holding students back.

Previously, as an assistant principal, he might have avoided this scenario or downplayed the issues, afraid that showing uncertainty would damage his credibility. But this time was different. Jamal had embraced the idea of "humble confidence." He understood that admitting uncertainty or acknowledging a challenge wouldn't weaken him; it would help build trust.

He began, "I know many of you are working hard to make the new reading curriculum more meaningful for our students. Some of you have found great successes, while others are still trying to find your footing. I want you to know that I don't have all the answers—I'm learning alongside you."

He paused, scanning the room, letting that truth settle. Then he continued, "I've seen some impressive small-group strategies, and I've also noticed areas where instruction can grow stronger. Rather than pretending I have a perfect formula, I'd like us to figure this out together. I'm confident in your expertise, and I'm confident that we have the collective strength to improve. At the same time, I know we'll need to make tough calls and confront practices that don't serve our students well. If I see something that concerns me, I promise to address it honestly—but I'll do it by listening, asking questions, and collaborating to find a better way. I may not have all the solutions, but I'm committed to seeking them with you."

There was a moment of quiet. Instead of polite nods or uneasy shifts, a sense of relief spread across the room. Teachers recognized that Jamal wasn't positioning himself as the all-knowing problem-solver, nor was he sidestepping accountability. He was leading from a place of authenticity—steady, open, and ready to lean on the faculty's collective wisdom.

Over the following weeks, when Jamal met with individual teachers to discuss reading instruction, his approach reflected the balance he'd promised. If he was uncertain about a particular intervention's effectiveness, he said so. Then he would invite the teacher to brainstorm alternatives. When he needed to point out a shortfall—like a reliance on worksheets that didn't deepen comprehension—he did it with candor and care, making it clear that this wasn't about blame but about growing together.

Teachers started coming to him with questions and solutions of their own. Because Jamal showed that humility and confidence could coexist, faculty members felt safer admitting their struggles and experimenting with new techniques. They knew Jamal believed in them enough to share responsibility and high expectations, all while standing beside them, shoulder to shoulder, in the effort to improve.

In this way, the theories from Chapter Two came to life. By blending self-assurance with vulnerability, Jamal became a leader who didn't need a façade of perfection. His humble confidence encouraged a culture of trust, honest dialogue, and continuous growth at Pine Grove Middle School.

CHAPTER THREE

The Cost of Perfectionism: Why Leaders Need to Let Go

The pursuit of excellence is a defining feature of most great leaders. In many ways, striving to do things well, set high standards, and work with diligence are all valuable traits that push leaders to achieve remarkable results. But when that drive morphs into perfectionism, it becomes an invisible force that can hold you back, drain your energy, and limit your team's potential. Perfectionism, at its core, is rooted in a need for control and a fear of failure, but it often results in just the opposite, stifling creativity, limiting collaboration, and creating an environment where fear of mistakes overshadows the pursuit of meaningful progress.

In this chapter, we'll examine the costs of perfectionism in leadership and why letting go of this unrealistic ideal can lead to more effective, sustainable, and rewarding leadership. We'll explore the impact perfectionism has on leaders themselves and on their teams, and we'll look at practical ways to embrace a mindset focused on growth, adaptability, and progress rather than flawless execution.

Understanding Perfectionism in Leadership

Perfectionism might appear to be about achieving high standards, but it's often much more complicated. Leaders driven by perfectionism feel the need to be seen as capable, knowledgeable, and worthy of their position. The stakes feel high; after all, in a school or organization, the well-being of students, staff, and the institution as a whole can seem to rest on every decision. But perfectionism is less about achieving excellence and more about fear—fear of mistakes, of judgment, of appearing inadequate.

For a leader, this can translate into micromanagement, reluctance to delegate, excessive self-criticism, and a lack of satisfaction even when things go well. Instead of creating a high-achieving environment, it creates a climate of stress and rigidity that can paralyze both the leader and the team.

The Hidden Costs of Perfectionism

The effects of perfectionism aren't always visible, but they're there—undermining productivity, eroding trust, and stifling growth. Here are a few of the most common, yet often unacknowledged, costs:

1. **Loss of Innovation and Creativity**

    When perfectionism is at play, every decision feels like it needs to be flawless, which can quickly shut down creativity and experimentation. The focus shifts to getting things "right" instead of trying new approaches or finding creative solutions. For leaders, this can mean holding back ideas that feel too risky or unconventional, and it can stifle their team's willingness to experiment as well. People are far less likely to take creative risks if they fear being judged for their ideas or feel that only "perfect" solutions are acceptable.

    For example, imagine a teacher who has an innovative idea for a new approach to student engagement but feels hesitant to share it because the plan isn't fully fleshed out. If a leader insists on perfection, that teacher may decide not to bring it up at all, potentially depriving students of a valuable, creative learning experience.

2. **Micromanagement and Burnout**

Perfectionism often leads to micromanagement. Leaders who struggle with perfectionism may have difficulty delegating tasks because they fear that others won't meet their standards. As a result, they end up shouldering too many responsibilities, working excessive hours, and eventually experiencing burnout. Not only is this unsustainable, but it also sends the message to the team that they aren't trusted or capable of handling key responsibilities.

Micromanagement doesn't just take a toll on the leader—it affects team morale, too. When team members feel that their leader doesn't trust them to do their jobs, they become disengaged and less motivated. People want to feel empowered and respected in their roles, and a micromanaging leader stifles that sense of autonomy.

> People want to feel empowered and respected in their roles, and a micromanaging leader stifles that sense of autonomy.

3. **Fear-Based Culture**

Perfectionism can unintentionally create a culture of fear. When leaders set unrealistically high expectations and focus on avoiding mistakes at all costs, team members may become afraid of taking risks, speaking up, or making decisions independently. They may worry that even minor errors will lead to harsh criticism or judgment, which can create an environment in which everyone is more focused on not failing than on making progress.

This fear-based culture can be particularly damaging in educational settings, where open dialogue, creativity, and adaptability are essential for effective teaching and learning. When teachers and staff feel they can't make mistakes, they may hold back from trying new approaches or challenging the status quo—ultimately limiting the growth and potential of the entire organization.

4. **Stunted Personal and Professional Growth**

Ironically, perfectionism hinders the very growth it's supposed to encourage. When leaders are overly focused on avoiding mistakes, they miss out on valuable learning experiences. Mistakes and failures are essential opportunities for growth, self-reflection, and improvement. A leader who is unwilling to acknowledge their imperfections deprives themselves of these opportunities, stunting their personal and professional development.

In addition, when leaders present an image of perfection, it can prevent others from offering constructive feedback. If the team perceives the leader as unapproachable or defensive about their decisions, they may withhold feedback that could help the leader grow and improve.

Letting Go of Perfectionism: Embracing Progress and Growth

Letting go of perfectionism doesn't mean lowering standards or becoming careless. Rather, it's about shifting the focus from flawless execution to continuous improvement, learning, and growth. Here are some strategies for adopting a healthier, more balanced approach to leadership:

1. **Embrace Mistakes and Feedback as Tools for Growth**

One of the most effective ways to let go of perfectionism is to shift your perspective on mistakes and feedback. Instead of viewing mistakes as failures, see them as valuable learning opportunities that can guide you toward better outcomes. As a leader, your response to mistakes sets the tone for your team. When you openly acknowledge your own missteps and share what you've learned, you create a culture in which mistakes are seen as steppingstones, rather than obstacles, to success.

For example, suppose your team rolls out a new student behavior intervention plan, but after a few weeks, you realize it isn't working as expected. Instead of labeling it a failure, reframe it as an opportunity to refine the approach: "We've learned that this strategy isn't as effective as we hoped, but now we have a better understanding of what our students need. Let's adjust our approach based on what we've observed." This mindset fosters resilience and encourages innovation.

In the same way, actively seeking and embracing feedback is crucial to growth. Encourage your team to share constructive feedback and model how to receive it with openness. When leaders treat feedback as a gift rather than a critique, it empowers others to speak up and contribute to meaningful improvements.

2. Set Realistic Goals and Celebrate Progress

Perfectionism often leads to frustration because it sets an impossible standard where nothing ever feels "good enough." Instead, set realistic, achievable goals and broaden your definition of success to include effort, learning, and progress. Success doesn't mean everything goes perfectly the first time—it means you are moving forward and improving over time.

For example, if your team has been working on improving student engagement, take the time to recognize their efforts even if the overall engagement numbers aren't where you ultimately want them to be. Acknowledge small victories, such as a teacher successfully trying out a new instructional strategy that sparked more student participation. Saying something like, "I saw the way your students were engaged during your lesson today—it's clear that your new approach is making a difference" can go a long way in maintaining motivation and reinforcing a growth mindset.

3. Delegate and Empower Others

A major contributor to perfectionism is the belief that everything must be done personally to ensure it's done "right." However, effective leadership is about empowering others, trusting them to contribute, and understanding that different approaches can still lead to success. Delegating tasks allows leaders to focus on higher-level priorities while fostering growth and responsibility among team members.

For example, if a teacher is leading a parent engagement event, instead of dictating every detail, give them the autonomy to plan it in their own way. Offer guidance if they ask for it but allow them the space to bring their own creativity and ideas to the process. Even if their approach differs from how you would do it, trust that it can still be effective.

Recognizing and appreciating team members for their contributions strengthens trust and reinforces their confidence. A simple acknowledgment— "I really appreciate how you took the lead on that project. Your approach brought fresh ideas that made it even better"— can build morale and encourage continued leadership.

By embracing mistakes and feedback, setting realistic goals while celebrating progress, and delegating responsibilities to empower your team, leaders can move away from perfectionism and foster a more resilient, motivated, and growth-oriented culture.

Conclusion: Embracing Imperfection to Lead with Authenticity

The cost of perfectionism in leadership is high, but letting go of this unrealistic ideal opens the door to more sustainable, effective, and authentic leadership. By shifting your focus from flawless execution to continuous growth, you not only relieve yourself of unnecessary stress but also create an environment in which others feel empowered to take risks, make mistakes, and learn alongside you. Leading with authenticity means embracing your humanity—imperfections and all—and allowing others to do the same.

> Leading with authenticity means embracing your humanity—imperfections and all—and allowing others to do the same.

As you continue on your leadership journey, remember that letting go of perfectionism isn't about lowering your standards; it's about redefining what success means. True success in leadership isn't about doing everything perfectly; it's about learning, growing, and building a community where everyone is encouraged to bring their whole selves to the table. By cultivating a mindset focused on progress, resilience, and adaptability, you lead with strength and inspire those around you to strive not for perfection, but for growth.

As we delve into Chapter Four, we'll discuss the art of listening to criticism with intention, viewing it as a pathway to deeper self-awareness and professional development. We'll cover strategies for receiving feedback without defensiveness, evaluating criticism objectively, and transforming feedback into actionable steps for improvement. You'll learn how to cultivate a feedback-friendly culture within your team, where constructive criticism is welcomed and encouraged at every level.

By embracing feedback as an opportunity for growth rather than as a judgment, you'll develop the resilience and adaptability necessary to lead authentically. Embracing criticism with grace and a willingness to learn doesn't just make you a better leader; it sets a powerful example for your team, fostering a culture where everyone is committed to self-improvement, openness, and mutual respect.

Let's take this next step together, as we explore how listening to the voices around you—especially when it's hard—can turn your weaknesses into strengths and propel you toward your full potential as a leader.

Self-Reflection Prompt

As you consider the impact of perfectionism on your leadership, think about how it has influenced your decisions, relationships, and approach to challenges. Reflect on moments when striving for flawlessness may have led to frustration or limited your openness to new ideas. Consider both the direct and indirect effects of this mindset on your team or organization.

Reflection Question

Can you recall a recent situation where your desire for perfection held you or your team back? What would have happened if you had approached the situation with a focus on progress rather than perfection? How might this change have affected both your stress level and the outcomes for your team?

Write your reflections, and use them as a guide to approach future challenges with a mindset that values growth, adaptability, and shared learning over flawless execution.

LESSONS LEARNED

Arianna had always prided herself on setting high standards. As the principal of Maplewood Elementary, she believed her relentless pursuit of excellence ensured that every classroom hummed with rigor and efficiency. Every hallway bulletin board, every lesson plan, every schedule—Arianna insisted on perfection. At first, it seemed admirable: the school's test scores were consistently above average, the building looked immaculate, and parents praised Maplewood's organization.

But over time, Arianna began to notice cracks beneath the polished surface. Teachers seemed tense and drained, whispering warily in the hallways after school. Staff turnover was inching up, and some of her most talented teachers had started seeking transfers. When a veteran teacher quietly mentioned feeling "exhausted" and "unsupported," Arianna was taken aback. Wasn't she giving them everything they needed—carefully curated resources, detailed directives, and precise expectations?

One Wednesday afternoon, as Arianna hurried through the corridors checking up on a new literacy initiative, she found Ms. Baker, a normally upbeat second-grade teacher, in her classroom well past dismissal. Ms. Baker looked close to tears, sorting through a pile of unfinished grading rubrics. Arianna asked what was wrong, and Ms. Baker hesitated before answering. Finally, she admitted that the relentless push for perfection—the polished lesson plans, the immaculate data charts, the never-mistake-ready classroom environment—was wearing everyone down. The teachers felt no room to try something new, experiment, or ask for help without appearing weak or behind. They were too busy polishing the surface to risk learning from mistakes.

Arianna left that conversation troubled. She'd never intended to create such pressure. She wanted Maplewood to be excellent, but at what cost? That evening, she mulled over the idea that perfectionism might be robbing teachers of their creativity and resilience. Instead of fostering a community of learners—adults and kids alike—she'd built a tightly controlled environment where fear of error trumped curiosity and growth.

Over the next few weeks, Arianna made a conscious shift. In staff meetings, she acknowledged the toll that perfectionism had taken. "I realize that I've been pushing us to get everything exactly right, all the time," she told the faculty gathered in the media center. "I see now that this can make it hard to take risks or try new approaches. From now on, I want us to remember that progress matters more than perfection. Mistakes aren't failures; they're steppingstones to learning."

Her words were met with a quiet sigh of relief—and a few stunned expressions. Arianna followed through by encouraging teachers to share ideas that weren't fully formed and to talk openly about what wasn't working. Instead of expecting every unit plan to be flawless before it was taught, she invited teachers to reflect afterward, refining as they went. She started praising not just results, but also the willingness to try something different, even if it didn't pan out perfectly.

The changes weren't instant, but they were noticeable eventually. Within a month, staff meetings took on a more collaborative tone. A new reading strategy Ms. Baker tested wasn't flawless at first—it needed tweaks—but Arianna's response was gratitude and interest: "What did we learn this week? How can we adjust for next time?" Rather than punishing the shortfalls, Arianna celebrated the insights gained from trying. Teacher morale began to lift, and a sense of authentic collegiality took root.

As the year progressed, educators at Maplewood Elementary still cared about quality, but perfection no longer reigned supreme. Teachers felt freer to innovate, students sensed the positive energy, and Arianna herself felt less burdened by constant vigilance. By letting go of the need for flawlessness, she gave her school a powerful gift: the room to grow, improve, and become stronger over time.

In this way, the lessons of Chapter Three came to life. By acknowledging the cost of perfectionism and learning to let go, Arianna transformed her leadership and her school's culture, making Maplewood a place where striving for better—not perfect—fueled continuous growth and resilience.

CHAPTER FOUR

Listening to Criticism: Turning Weaknesses into Growth Opportunities

As leaders, we often find ourselves in the position of giving feedback to those we lead—guiding teachers, mentoring staff, and helping them improve. But when it comes to receiving feedback ourselves, especially critical feedback, the process can make us feel far more vulnerable. Criticism can be hard to hear, even when it's constructive. It challenges our self-image, pushes us out of our comfort zone, and sometimes feels like a personal attack rather than an opportunity for growth. Yet, learning to embrace feedback is one of the most transformative skills a leader can develop.

This chapter is about redefining our relationship with criticism, viewing it not as a threat to our competence or authority but as a gift—a source of valuable insights that can help us recognize and address our weaknesses. Leaders who actively listen to feedback, especially the hard truths, not only improve their own effectiveness but also create a culture of openness and trust. In this chapter, we'll explore the value of constructive criticism, strategies for receiving it with grace, and methods for transforming it into meaningful growth. By approaching feedback with curiosity and humility, you'll not only grow as a leader but set a powerful example for those around you.

Why Listening to Criticism Matters in Leadership

Criticism, especially when it's directed at something we care about deeply, can be painful. For leaders, criticism often feels particularly high-stakes because we're responsible not only for our own actions but for the impact we have on others. However, criticism—when constructive—offers us something priceless: the opportunity to understand how our leadership style affects those around us and to recognize areas we may have overlooked. Constructive criticism gives you the opportunity to:

- **Uncover blind spots**: There may be aspects of your leadership that impact your team in ways you hadn't realized. Criticism reveals these hidden areas, allowing you to make adjustments.
- **Enhance trust and connection**: Leaders who accept and act on feedback show their teams that they're open to growth, creating a culture where others feel safe to share their own feedback.
- **Drive continuous improvement**: Criticism can highlight specific areas where growth is needed, helping you refine your approach and become a more effective leader.
- **Model humility and resilience**: By accepting criticism with grace, you model an essential quality of good leadership: the ability to learn and adapt.

As challenging as it may be to accept, criticism is one of the most powerful tools for improvement. The key is to approach it with the right mindset, viewing it as a learning opportunity rather than a personal judgment.

Changing Your Mindset About Criticism

To truly benefit from criticism, it's essential to adopt a mindset that welcomes feedback rather than dreads it. This shift requires us to see criticism as a natural and necessary part of growth. Here's how to start changing your relationship with feedback:

1. **Separate Ego from Evaluation**

    One of the most significant obstacles to accepting criticism is our ego. When we identify too closely with our role or position, any critique of our actions can feel like a critique of our worth. To receive criticism effectively, practice separating your sense of self-worth from the feedback. Instead of viewing criticism as an attack, see it as an objective evaluation of specific actions or decisions.

    For example, if someone mentions that you tend to dominate discussions in meetings, don't let your ego interpret it as a comment on your value as a leader. Instead, view it as useful data about your communication style, something you can work on without questioning your worth.

2. **Reframe Feedback as a Gift**

    It can help to remember that feedback, especially when given thoughtfully, is a gift. It takes courage for others to voice their perspectives, particularly when they feel a critique might upset you. If a colleague, team member, or supervisor offers constructive criticism, it's likely because they believe in your potential and want to help you grow.

    The next time you receive feedback, try responding with gratitude, even if the message is difficult to hear. Thank the person for their honesty and willingness to share their thoughts. This simple act of appreciation will not only improve your mindset, but also reinforce that you value their input.

3. See Criticism as a Path to Mastery

Mastering any skill—whether in leadership, teaching, or any other field—requires a willingness to learn from both successes and mistakes. Criticism is one of the most valuable tools in this process. It serves as a mirror, reflecting areas that may need adjustment, refinement, or a fresh approach. Rather than viewing criticism as a personal attack, reframing it as a guidepost on the road to mastery can shift your entire perspective.

True mastery is not achieved in isolation. It is cultivated through a cycle of action, reflection, feedback, and improvement. Criticism, when approached with the right mindset, becomes a vital part of this cycle. It highlights blind spots we may not see on our own and offers insights that can accelerate our growth. When we choose to listen with curiosity instead of defensiveness, we unlock the potential for deeper development.

Think of criticism as the voice of a coach who is invested in your success. Great athletes depend on their coaches to analyze their performance, identify weaknesses, and push them to become better. Similarly, effective leaders lean into feedback from colleagues, mentors, and even those they lead. Each observation, whether positive or critical, becomes another step toward leadership excellence.

> **Think of criticism as the voice of a coach who is invested in your success.**

The path to mastery is not about perfection—it's about progress. Each piece of feedback is a gift that can move you forward. When you view criticism through this lens, it becomes less of a threat and more of an invitation to grow into the leader you are capable of becoming.

Strategies for Receiving Criticism with Grace

Once you've cultivated a mindset that embraces criticism, the next step is to develop practical strategies for receiving it constructively. Here are several techniques that can help you listen to criticism without feeling defensive or overwhelmed:

1. **Listen Actively and Without Interruption**

    When someone offers feedback, let them speak fully before responding. Resist the urge to jump in, defend yourself, or clarify your intentions. Instead, listen actively, focusing on understanding the content of the feedback. Use non-verbal cues, like nodding or maintaining eye contact, to show that you're engaged and receptive.

    For example, if a teacher is providing feedback about your decision-making process, listen carefully to their perspective without interrupting. They may feel more comfortable sharing their thoughts when they know you're listening attentively.

2. **Ask Clarifying Questions**

    Once the person has finished speaking, ask clarifying questions if needed. This not only helps you understand the feedback fully but also shows that you're genuinely interested in their perspective. Avoid questions that sound defensive, such as *"Why do you feel that way?"* Instead, try questions like, *"Can you give me an example of when this happened?"* or *"How would you suggest approaching this differently?"*

    These questions signal that you're open to learning from the feedback and that you value the person's insights.

3. **Pause Before Responding**

    After listening and asking clarifying questions, take a brief pause before responding. This moment of reflection allows you to process the feedback and avoid reacting emotionally. A simple *"Thank you for *sharing that with me. I appreciate it"* can go a long way in showing your openness, even if you're still processing.

If the feedback is particularly challenging, you might say, *"Thank you for your honesty. I'd like to take some time to reflect on this and will get back to you."* This approach gives you space to think about the feedback without feeling pressured to respond immediately.

4. **Avoid Defensiveness**

Defensiveness is a natural reaction to criticism, but it can create unnecessary tension and prevent you from fully understanding the feedback. Instead of defending yourself, acknowledge the feedback openly. If the feedback feels inaccurate, you can still respond with a neutral, reflective approach.

For instance, if you feel the criticism doesn't align with your intentions, say something like, *"Thank you for letting me know how this came across. I'll reflect on how I could have communicated differently."* This response shows that you're taking the feedback seriously, even if you don't entirely agree with it.

5. **Reflect and Act on the Feedback**

Once you've received the feedback, take time to reflect on it privately. Ask yourself: What specific actions can I take to address this? Are there adjustments I can make to my behavior, communication style, or approach? Reflect on the broader patterns or lessons the feedback might reveal.

After reflecting, set specific, actionable goals for improvement. For example, if the feedback was about your tendency to rush decisions, you might set a goal to include key team members in the decision-making process more regularly. Taking action shows that you're committed to growth and reinforces to your team that their feedback matters.

Turning Criticism into Growth Opportunities

Receiving feedback is only the first step; the real value lies in transforming it into tangible growth. Here's how to turn criticism into a tool for continuous improvement:

1. **Identify Patterns and Areas for Development**

   As you receive feedback over time, look for recurring themes or patterns. If you notice similar comments from multiple sources, it may indicate an area where growth is needed. For example, if you frequently hear that you come across as unapproachable, consider strategies to make yourself more accessible, such as holding regular office hours for your team. By recognizing patterns, you can pinpoint areas for development and address them proactively, rather than waiting for issues to escalate.

2. **Set Concrete Goals Based on Feedback**

   Once you've identified areas for improvement, set specific, measurable goals to address them. For example, if you received feedback about being overly critical in meetings, set a goal to offer at least two positive comments for every piece of constructive feedback. By creating actionable goals, you can track your progress and make tangible improvements.

3. **Seek Ongoing Feedback to Measure Progress**

   Growth is an ongoing process, so seek additional feedback as you work on your development goals. Ask your team or colleagues if they've noticed any changes in the areas you're working on. This demonstrates your commitment to improvement and provides valuable insights into your progress.

   For example, you might say, "I've been working on being more open in meetings. Have you noticed any difference?" By inviting continued feedback, you reinforce a culture of openness and show that you're serious about becoming the best leader you can be.

4. **Express Gratitude for Constructive Criticism**

When people give you honest feedback, they're investing in your growth. Show your appreciation by thanking them for their insights, both in the moment and as you make progress. A simple, "Thank you for helping me grow" goes a long way in building trust and encouraging others to share feedback in the future.

Conclusion: Embracing Feedback as a Path to Growth

Listening to criticism is one of the most difficult, yet most transformative, skills a leader can cultivate. When you approach feedback as a tool for improvement rather than as a personal judgment, you unlock new levels of self-awareness, resilience, and effectiveness. Criticism reveals areas for growth, helps you connect more authentically with those you lead, and builds a culture of trust, where everyone feels valued and empowered to share their perspectives.

By listening to the hard truths others share, you're not only growing as a leader—you're setting an example of humility, adaptability, and strength. Embracing feedback allows you to refine your approach, learn from your mistakes, and continuously improve, creating a legacy of leadership built on openness and mutual respect.

As you grow in self-awareness and learn from constructive criticism, you're also ready to take on one of the most empowering aspects of leadership: *delegation*. In the next chapter, we'll explore the importance of knowing your limits and the art of empowering others by entrusting them with responsibility. We'll discuss how effective delegation not only lightens your own load but also builds confidence, skill, and ownership within your team.

Chapter Five will guide you through the mindset, strategies, and techniques for sharing leadership so you can foster a collaborative environment where everyone has the opportunity to grow and contribute. By learning to delegate effectively, you'll unlock your team's potential, strengthen your organization's capacity, and create a balanced, sustainable approach to leadership.

Self-Reflection Prompt

Reflect on your recent experiences with receiving feedback, especially if it challenged you or highlighted areas for improvement. Consider how you felt in the moment and how you processed the feedback afterward. Think about any patterns in your reactions—whether defensive, open, or somewhere in between.

Reflection Question

Can you recall a specific instance when constructive criticism helped you grow as a leader? What was your initial reaction, and how did you ultimately turn the feedback into an opportunity for improvement? If you struggled to accept it, what could you do differently next time to approach criticism as a valuable tool for growth? Take time to write your thoughts, and consider how embracing a mindset of openness to feedback can deepen your leadership effectiveness and relationships with your team.

LESSONS LEARNED

Dr. Patel had been superintendent of Riverbend Unified School District for nearly two years. When she assumed the role, she arrived with a solid track record from her previous position, a glowing recommendation from the board, and a strategic plan aimed at closing achievement gaps, improving staff retention, and enhancing community engagement. On paper, everything looked promising.

Yet recently, something felt amiss. Parent turnout at town hall sessions was dwindling, teacher morale seemed shaky, and she'd received a few pointed emails from staff about "communication issues." These critiques were vague enough that Dr. Patel could have dismissed them as a few disgruntled voices. But she knew from experience that smoke often signaled fire.

After a restless weekend wrestling with these nagging doubts, Dr. Patel decided to seek candid feedback. She reached out to a cross-section of district stakeholders: teachers, support staff, principals, and a group of parents active in the PTA. She invited them to a series of informal listening sessions, making it clear that she wanted to hear not just what was working, but what wasn't.

The first few meetings were polite but guarded. Teachers hesitated, occasionally exchanging glances as though silently asking, *Is it really safe to speak up?* Dr. Patel understood their caution. Superintendents held a lot of power. She realized she needed to show genuine openness, not just say the words. When one teacher, Mr. Carrillo, finally voiced that the district's communication about new curriculum standards had felt top-down and rushed, Dr. Patel resisted the urge to explain or defend. Instead, she thanked him and asked for an example. He described a moment when he and his colleagues learned about a significant shift in testing protocols only days before a staff training—leaving them feeling unprepared and undervalued.

Another participant, a parent named Ms. Jenkins, mentioned how school newsletters and website updates often lacked practical information about how new district initiatives would affect their children's day-to-day experience. She said parents felt "in the dark," uncertain about how these changes helped or hindered their students.

A principal, Dr. Song, expressed that while she admired the district's ambitious goals, the relentless pace of adopting new programs without soliciting building-level input made it hard for principals to plan effectively. It felt like they were always scrambling to keep up, rather than thoughtfully guiding improvements in their schools.

As Dr. Patel listened, she felt a twinge of defensiveness tugging at her. She wanted to explain the reasons behind the tight timelines or emphasize the district's resource constraints. But she recalled the chapter's lessons: to approach criticism as a gift, an opportunity to see blind spots and grow stronger. So she pressed on with curiosity. She asked each person, "What do you think could help us communicate better?" and "How might we give schools more voice in these decisions?"

Their suggestions were concrete and actionable. Teachers wanted regular, two-way communication channels—perhaps a quarterly "curriculum roundtable" where teacher leaders, principals, and district staff could preview changes together. Parents proposed a simpler, more transparent communication plan that translated district decisions into "what this means for your child" bullet points. Principals suggested a rotating advisory committee that would review major initiatives well in advance, providing feedback before they rolled out.

None of the critique Dr. Patel heard that week felt good in the moment—criticism rarely does. But taking it in without rushing to defend her choices gave her a clearer picture of the district's weaknesses and how to address them. It also showed her team, staff, and parents that she wasn't just inviting feedback as a formality—she was willing to hear it, learn from it, and adapt.

In the months that followed, Dr. Patel implemented several of the suggestions: the curriculum roundtables became a reality, co-designed by teachers and district staff. A simplified communication template for district decisions went home to parents each month. An advisory council of principals met quarterly with her cabinet to discuss upcoming proposals. Gradually, the tone of the feedback shifted. People noticed changes and acknowledged them. Instead of grumbling in private, stakeholders began bringing their insights and ideas to the new channels Dr. Patel had created.

By listening to criticism and embracing her weaknesses, Dr. Patel turned a tense, uncertain moment into a catalyst for improvement. Her district grew not in spite of the criticism, but because of it—more transparent, more collaborative, and more aligned with the people it served. In this way, the lessons from Chapter Four sprang to life: feedback, even when uncomfortable, proved to be the key that unlocked stronger relationships, wiser decisions, and a more resilient educational community.

CHAPTER FIVE

Delegate, Don't Dominate: Recognizing When to Step Back

You don't know everything, you're not good at everything, in fact, someone on your team is probably more skilled in _____ than YOU! I know it stings, but get over yourself!

One of the most significant, yet often challenging, responsibilities of a leader is delegation. Many leaders find themselves juggling countless tasks and decisions, often feeling that they alone must handle each of these challenges. However, effective leadership is not about shouldering every responsibility; it's about recognizing your limits, knowing when to step back, and empowering others to take on meaningful roles.

Delegation is an essential skill that allows leaders to maximize their impact while developing the strengths of those around them. But true delegation isn't merely about handing off tasks. It's about fostering trust, encouraging independence, and giving your team the space to contribute their unique skills and ideas. When leaders master the art of delegation, they not only alleviate their own burdens but also create a thriving, dynamic team empowered to rise to new challenges.

In this chapter, we'll explore the importance of delegation in leadership, discuss why leaders often resist it, and provide practical strategies to delegate effectively. By learning to share responsibilities, you'll become a stronger, more balanced leader, one who cultivates a collaborative environment where everyone can grow and succeed.

The Importance of Delegation in Leadership

Delegation is more than just a time-management tool; it's a fundamental aspect of effective leadership. When done thoughtfully, delegation builds trust, drives productivity, and strengthens the overall organization. Here are some of the key benefits of delegating:

1. **Fostering Trust and Team Growth**

    Delegation is a powerful tool for building a culture of trust within your team. When you assign meaningful responsibilities, you signal that you believe in your team's abilities and judgment. This vote of confidence serves as a motivator, encouraging team members to take ownership of their work and perform at their best. Trust creates an environment in which individuals feel valued and empowered, leading to greater job satisfaction and stronger commitment to the organization's success.

    Beyond trust, delegation also fuels team growth. By assigning new tasks and leadership opportunities, you offer team members valuable learning experiences. They gain new skills, develop their problem-solving abilities, and grow their confidence. As individuals strengthen their

> As individuals strengthen their capabilities, the collective expertise of the team expands.

capabilities, the collective expertise of the team expands. This diversity of skills enhances your organization's capacity to tackle complex challenges and seize new opportunities.

2. **Enhancing Resilience and Adaptability**

A team overly reliant on a single leader for guidance is vulnerable to disruption. When every decision flows through one person, the organization's progress can stall during times of absence, crisis, or transition. Delegation mitigates this risk by distributing responsibility across the team. When individuals are entrusted with tasks and encouraged to make decisions, they develop the capability to navigate challenges independently.

This process fosters resilience—a team's ability to withstand and recover from setbacks. It also cultivates adaptability. When team members are equipped to step into different roles and respond to changing circumstances, the organization becomes more agile. Delegation ensures that your team is not just prepared for today's demands but is also capable of evolving and thriving in the face of future uncertainties.

3. **Preserving Leadership Capacity and Well-Being**

Effective leaders understand that their greatest impact comes from focusing on what only they can do. When leaders attempt to manage every detail, they risk being consumed by day-to-day operations, leaving little room for strategic thinking and long-term vision. Delegation allows you to reclaim your time and direct your energy toward the big-picture responsibilities that drive organizational growth—such as setting direction, shaping culture, and pursuing innovation.

Moreover, delegation is essential for maintaining your well-being. Leaders who try to carry every burden often face burnout—marked by exhaustion, stress, and diminishing effectiveness. Sharing the load helps you maintain a sustainable pace, ensuring you remain energized and capable of leading with clarity and purpose. This balance also models healthy work habits for your team, fostering an environment where well-being is valued and prioritized.

Why Leaders Struggle to Delegate

Despite the many benefits of delegation, many leaders find it difficult to let go of tasks and responsibilities. Understanding why you may resist delegation can help you overcome these obstacles. Here are a few common reasons leaders struggle with delegation:

1. **Fear of Losing Control**

One of the biggest psychological barriers to delegation is the fear of losing control. Many leaders believe that if they personally oversee every task, they can ensure things are done correctly and efficiently. However, this mindset can lead to micromanagement, which not only stifles the development of team members but also drains the leader's own time and energy. When leaders hold on too tightly, they inadvertently create a bottleneck—slowing progress and overwhelming themselves with responsibilities.

Instead of viewing delegation as a loss of control, leaders should see it as an opportunity to empower others. By setting clear expectations, providing guidance, and establishing accountability measures, leaders can maintain quality while giving their team members room to grow. Delegation doesn't mean relinquishing responsibility—it means trusting others to take ownership while still providing oversight.

2. **Perfectionism**

Leaders who have high personal standards often struggle to delegate because they fear others won't meet those same expectations. They may worry that mistakes will be made or that the final outcome won't be as polished as if they had done it themselves. While aiming for excellence is admirable, perfectionism can create an unsustainable workload and limit the team's ability to function independently.

Perfectionism can also erode trust and morale within a team. If employees feel that nothing they do is ever "good enough," they may become disengaged or hesitant to take initiative. Leaders must learn to distinguish between tasks that truly require perfection and those where "good enough" is actually sufficient. By focusing on outcomes rather than rigid processes, leaders can help their teams develop skills, confidence, and a sense of ownership over their work.

3. Belief in Personal Responsibility

A strong sense of responsibility is often what makes someone a great leader—but when taken to an extreme, it can also be a leader's downfall. Some leaders feel that their organization's success rests solely on their shoulders, making it difficult to delegate tasks without feeling like they're neglecting their duties. They may believe that asking for help is a sign of weakness or that they must personally oversee every detail to ensure success.

However, effective leadership is not about doing everything alone; it's about cultivating a team that can function collaboratively toward shared goals. By holding onto too much responsibility, leaders risk burnout and create an environment where their team members feel underutilized. True leadership involves recognizing that delegation is not a failure—it's a strategic move that strengthens the organization by allowing others to contribute meaningfully.

> True leadership involves recognizing that delegation is not a failure—it's a strategic move that strengthens the organization by allowing others to contribute meaningfully.

4. **Lack of Trust in Others' Abilities**

Many leaders hesitate to delegate because they're unsure if their team members have the skills or experience needed to handle certain tasks. This lack of trust often stems from limited exposure to their team's capabilities or past experiences where delegation didn't go as planned. However, without opportunities to take on new challenges, employees can't develop the skills necessary to perform at a higher level.

Building trust requires intentional effort. Leaders should start by delegating smaller, low-risk tasks and providing clear instructions and feedback. As team members demonstrate competence, leaders can gradually increase their level of responsibility. Encouraging open communication, offering constructive feedback, and recognizing employees' strengths can help create a culture of trust where delegation becomes a natural and beneficial process.

By addressing these common delegation barriers, leaders can create a healthier, more efficient work environment. The key is to shift from a mindset of control to one of empowerment—ensuring that both leaders and their teams can thrive.

Practical Strategies for Effective Delegation

Effective delegation requires thoughtful planning, clear communication, and a willingness to let go. Here are some strategies to help you delegate tasks in a way that benefits both you and your team:

1. **Identify Tasks to Delegate**

Begin by identifying tasks or responsibilities that can be delegated. Consider routine tasks, projects that others are capable of handling, and activities that do not require your direct involvement. When you delegate these tasks, you'll free up time to focus on high-priority areas where your input is essential. Ask yourself:

- *Which tasks don't require my unique expertise or leadership?*
- *Are there tasks that someone else on my team might even be better suited to handle?*
- *Where can I make the most significant impact if I free up time from routine tasks?*

2. **Choose the Right People for the Right Tasks**

Successful delegation involves assigning tasks to team members whose skills and strengths align with the requirements of the project. Consider each person's unique abilities, interests, and growth potential. By matching the right people with the right tasks, you create opportunities for skill-building while ensuring the work is completed effectively.

For example, if you have a team member with strong organizational skills, consider delegating a project that requires detailed planning and coordination. By leveraging each person's strengths, you'll set your team up for success.

3. **Communicate Expectations Clearly**

Once you've decided to delegate a task, communicate your expectations clearly. This includes outlining the goals, deadlines, resources, and any specific guidelines for completing the work. Providing clarity at the outset helps avoid misunderstandings and empowers team members to work independently without constantly seeking guidance.

When delegating, consider framing expectations in terms of desired outcomes rather than specific steps. This gives team members the freedom to approach the task in their own way while still aligning with your vision.

4. **Provide the Necessary Resources and Support**

Delegation isn't about leaving someone to fend for themselves; it's about providing the support they need to succeed. Ensure that team members have access to the resources, training, and information necessary to complete the task. Let them know they can come to you with questions, but encourage them to problem-solve independently as well.

For example, if you're asking a team member to take on a new role in a project, consider offering them a mentor or connecting them with resources that can help them succeed. By setting them up with the tools they need, you'll build their confidence and capability.

5. **Encourage Ownership and Autonomy**

Effective delegation involves granting team members a sense of ownership over their work. Instead of micromanaging, allow them the autonomy to make decisions, solve problems, and take creative approaches. This autonomy not only boosts motivation but also allows team members to develop confidence in their abilities.

For instance, if you've assigned a teacher to lead a professional development workshop, encourage them to design the content in a way that reflects their unique strengths and insights. Give them the freedom to make the workshop their own, and they'll approach the task with greater enthusiasm and commitment.

6. **Follow Up and Offer Constructive Feedback**

While autonomy is important, so is accountability. After delegating a task, schedule regular check-ins to discuss progress, address any challenges, and offer constructive feedback. These check-ins provide an opportunity to celebrate successes, make course corrections if needed, and ensure that team members are on track to achieve the desired outcome.

Remember, feedback should be specific, actionable, and focused on growth. Constructive feedback reinforces positive behaviors and helps team members improve, while also showing that you're invested in their success.

7. Acknowledge and Celebrate Contributions

When team members take on responsibilities and meet or exceed expectations, acknowledge their hard work. Celebrating their achievements shows that you value their contributions and helps build a culture of appreciation. Public recognition not only boosts morale but also reinforces the importance of shared leadership.

For example, if a team member successfully completes a challenging project, take a moment to recognize their effort at a team meeting or through a personal note. Small gestures of appreciation go a long way in fostering loyalty, motivation, and pride in their work.

Conclusion: The Power of Shared Leadership

Delegation is not a sign of weakness; it's a testament to strong leadership. Leaders who recognize the value of stepping back allow others to step up, bringing diverse ideas, strengths, and perspectives to the organization. By trusting your team and sharing responsibility, you create a culture of collaboration, respect, and shared ownership.

Learning to delegate effectively is a journey that requires self-awareness, trust, and a willingness to let go. But as you begin to empower others and see them flourish, you'll realize that delegation is one of the most rewarding aspects of leadership. You're not only strengthening your organization; you're cultivating the next generation of leaders who will carry your mission forward.

By embracing shared leadership, you're creating an environment in which everyone feels empowered to contribute and grow. You're demonstrating that leadership isn't about control but about connection, trust, and mutual success. As you let go of the need to manage every detail, you'll find a new level of fulfillment in your role—one that allows you to lead with purpose, focus, and balance.

As you step into a more balanced, empowering style of leadership, the ability to manage your emotions becomes increasingly essential.

Leadership comes with its fair share of pressures and unexpected challenges, and how you respond emotionally sets the tone for your team. In the next chapter, we'll explore strategies for emotional regulation and the importance of modeling calmness in high-stress situations.

Chapter Six will provide practical techniques for managing stress, staying grounded, and remaining composed even when things don't go as planned. By mastering emotional resilience, you'll create an atmosphere of stability and trust, inspiring your team to stay focused and confident even in the face of adversity. Through emotional regulation, you'll reinforce your role as a leader who leads not only with strength but with poise, empathy, and unwavering composure.

Self-Reflection Prompt

Reflect on the roles and responsibilities you currently manage. Consider the areas where you feel stretched thin, where you're often the sole decision-maker, or where you've hesitated to hand tasks over to others. Think about how holding onto these responsibilities impacts your effectiveness and the development of those around you.

Reflection Question

Is there a recent situation where you could have delegated a task but chose not to? What were your reasons for keeping that responsibility? How might delegating this task have benefited both you and your team? Take some time to write your thoughts, and consider one or two areas where you could begin to step back and empower others. This practice can help you build trust within your team and create a more balanced approach to leadership.

LESSONS LEARNED

Monica had always defined her leadership as "leading from the front." As principal of Maplewood Intermediate, she took pride in her reputation for being everywhere at once. If a teacher needed new materials, Monica arranged the purchase herself. If a student's family required special support, Monica was on the phone with community agencies. When it came time to plan the school's annual literacy fair, she personally created the flyer, booked the presenters, and organized the volunteer schedule. Nothing escaped her eye.

But by winter of her third year, Monica found herself utterly drained. Each morning's to-do list was longer than the last, and she often left the building feeling as if she'd accomplished too little, despite never taking a break. Observing her carefully, the assistant principal, Ms. Nash, gently suggested that maybe the principal didn't need to oversee every detail. "You have capable staff who are eager to help," Ms. Nash said. "Let us share the load."

Monica resisted at first. How could she trust others to ensure the same level of quality and care that she brought? She'd seen too many leadership missteps before she came to Maplewood and was convinced that control guaranteed excellence. Yet, she couldn't deny that she was nearing burnout—and that her best intentions might be stifling the talents of those around her.

A turning point came just before the literacy fair. Monica was behind schedule on multiple projects—finalizing a hiring plan, meeting with a district supervisor about budget priorities, and preparing for a parent council meeting. The literacy fair was weeks away, and yet every decision, from which authors to invite to where to set up reading corners, sat on her desk, awaiting her final say.

Recognizing her own limitations, Monica decided to try something new. She called a brief meeting with a small team: a reading specialist known for her creativity, the media center coordinator who had community connections, a fifth-grade teacher experienced in managing parent volunteers, and Ms. Nash, her trusted assistant principal. Monica laid out the vision for the literacy fair: a welcoming, engaging event that celebrated reading and writing across all grade levels. Then she said words that felt almost foreign: "I'd like to hand this off to you. You know our students and families well. I trust you to bring this event to life."

At first, the team looked surprised. They'd grown accustomed to receiving orders from above. But as Monica explained the parameters, asked for their ideas, and encouraged them to make decisions, their surprise turned to excitement. Within days, the literacy fair team was meeting independently, discussing local authors they could invite, brainstorming interactive reading stations, and planning a schedule that gave each grade level a spotlight.

Monica still kept an eye on things, but from a distance.

When the team approached her to share an idea or seek feedback, she listened carefully and offered suggestions or guiding questions rather than directives. She asked, "How would families experience this new station?" or "What's your plan for handling large crowds?" Her approach shifted from commanding every detail to supporting the team's ownership and creativity.

On the night of the literacy fair, the school buzzed with energy. Parents strolled through hallways lined with student-written poetry. A local children's author signed copies of her latest book in the media center. Upper-grade students read aloud to younger peers in cozy reading nooks. Families left clutching recommended reading lists and smiling at the warm sense of community.

As the last visitors trickled out, Monica stood in the lobby, watching the team pack up. They were tired but exhilarated. The literacy specialist marveled at how smoothly the evening ran, and the teacher who managed parent volunteers grinned, noting how helpful and engaged everyone had been. Ms. Nash patted Monica on the shoulder, "This felt like the whole school came together. Delegating made a huge difference."

DELEGATE, DON'T DOMINATE

> Monica realized that by stepping back, she hadn't relinquished quality or influence—she had amplified it. Her staff, when given trust, tools, and the authority to act, rose to the challenge. In doing less herself, she had accomplished more for the school. The event felt richer and more authentic precisely because it showcased the team's collective strengths.
>
> After that night, Monica started rethinking her approach to leadership. She began delegating tasks and projects more frequently, ensuring everyone's workload was balanced and that people's unique talents were tapped. She noticed that without the weight of doing it all, she had more mental space to handle big-picture issues and long-term planning. Meanwhile, her staff developed newfound confidence and pride in their contributions.
>
> In this way, the lessons from Chapter Five took shape. By recognizing her limits and learning to let go, Monica elevated her leadership, empowered her team, and created a school environment where collaboration, trust, and shared purpose thrived.

CHAPTER SIX

Managing Emotions: Keeping Cool Under Pressure

Leadership often comes with high stakes, constant demands, and unexpected challenges. For those in charge, the ability to manage emotions effectively is as critical as technical skills or strategic thinking. Emotional regulation isn't about suppressing feelings or pretending to be unbothered; it's about recognizing, understanding, and controlling your emotional responses so that you can lead with clarity and confidence, even in stressful situations.

When leaders maintain calmness under pressure, they not only make better decisions but also model stability and resilience for their teams. In high-stress environments, emotions can quickly ripple out, affecting morale, productivity, and trust. By learning to manage emotions constructively, leaders create a supportive atmosphere where team members feel grounded, empowered, and motivated.

In this chapter, we'll explore the importance of emotional regulation in leadership, common emotional triggers, and strategies for staying composed during difficult moments. By mastering these techniques, you'll be able to handle challenges with poise and model a steady, resilient approach that encourages your team to do the same.

Why Emotional Regulation Matters in Leadership

Emotions play a powerful role in how we perceive situations, interact with others, and make decisions. When emotions are managed effectively, they provide valuable information and enhance our leadership. But when left unchecked, they can cloud judgment, strain relationships, and lead to impulsive decisions. Here's why emotional regulation is so crucial for leaders:

1. **Clear and Strategic Decision-Making**

    Effective leadership requires sound decision-making, especially in high-pressure situations. However, stress and heightened emotions can trigger reactive thinking, narrowing a leader's ability to see the full picture. When emotions dominate, decisions may be driven by fear, frustration, or urgency—resulting in short-term fixes that overlook long-term consequences.

    Emotionally regulated leaders, on the other hand, can pause, reflect, and gather the necessary information before acting. They create mental space to evaluate multiple options, anticipate potential outcomes, and align their choices with the team's vision and goals. This level-headed approach fosters confidence among team members, who see their leader as reliable and deliberate. It also invites collaboration, as people feel safe contributing ideas without the fear of emotional backlash.

    In the end, the leader's emotional steadiness ensures that decisions are not just quick—but wise, balanced, and forward-looking.

MANAGING EMOTIONS: KEEPING COOL UNDER PRESSURE

2. **Resilience and Adaptive Leadership**

Leadership is often defined not by how one performs when things are smooth, but by how one responds when things fall apart. Setbacks, uncertainties, and conflicts are inevitable in any organization. Emotionally reactive leaders may find themselves overwhelmed, demoralized, or prone to blame, which can stall progress and undermine morale.

> Leadership is often defined not by how one performs when things are smooth, but by how one responds when things fall apart.

Conversely, leaders who regulate their emotions demonstrate resilience—they can absorb challenges without becoming destabilized. They view difficulties as temporary hurdles rather than insurmountable failures. This mindset allows them to adapt quickly, pivot when needed, and maintain focus on solutions rather than problems. Their resilience also prevents negativity from spreading throughout the team.

When a leader maintains their composure and optimism during tough times, they inspire their teams to mirror that same resilience. Employees feel reassured that obstacles can be overcome, which fosters a culture of perseverance, creativity, and continuous improvement.

3. **Cultivating Trust and Stability in Teams**

A leader's emotional state profoundly influences the atmosphere of the entire team. When leaders are unpredictable, reactive, or quick to anger, it creates an environment of tension and insecurity. Team members may withdraw, avoid risks, or work defensively—fearing criticism or emotional outbursts.

Emotionally steady leaders, however, cultivate an atmosphere of psychological safety. They remain calm and composed, even under pressure, signaling to their teams that challenges are part of the process—not crises to be feared. Their behavior models that emotional stability is both possible and expected.

Additionally, these leaders demonstrate empathy and respect, especially during difficult times. They check in on their team's well-being, listen actively, and offer support without judgment. This builds trust and loyalty, as employees feel valued and understood.

Ultimately, when team members trust their leader's consistency and fairness, they are more likely to collaborate openly, take initiative, and invest fully in their work. The result is a team that is not only productive but also unified and resilient.

Common Emotional Triggers in Leadership

While every leader faces unique challenges, there are several common situations that can trigger strong emotional responses. Recognizing these triggers is the first step toward managing them constructively:

- **Unexpected Setbacks**: Whether it's a missed deadline, a sudden staffing change, or a policy shift, unexpected events can disrupt plans and create stress.
- **Criticism or Negative Feedback**: Criticism can feel personal, especially for leaders invested in their work. It's natural to feel defensive, but learning to view feedback objectively is essential.
- **High-Stakes Decisions**: When decisions have significant consequences, it's easy to feel overwhelmed or anxious about choosing the "right" path.
- **Conflicts within the Team**: Disagreements and interpersonal conflicts can strain relationships and create tension. Leaders are often responsible for resolving these conflicts, which can be emotionally taxing.
- **Pressure to Perform**: Leaders often feel the weight of expectation, both from others and from themselves. The pressure

to perform and achieve high standards can lead to stress and burnout.

Strategies for Managing Emotions in Leadership

Emotional regulation is a skill that can be developed with practice and intentionality. Here are several strategies for managing emotions effectively, so you can lead with composure and resilience:

1. **Practice Self-Awareness**

    The first step in managing emotions is to develop self-awareness. This means paying attention to your feelings, identifying patterns, and understanding how different situations affect you. By recognizing your emotional triggers, you can prepare yourself to respond more thoughtfully when they arise. Consider keeping a journal where you reflect on your emotional responses to various situations. After a challenging day, ask yourself:

    - *What emotions did I experience today, and what triggered them?*
    - *How did these emotions impact my thoughts, actions, and interactions with others?*
    - *Is there a recurring pattern I need to address?*

    Over time, this practice will help you develop greater self-awareness, making it easier to catch emotional reactions early and manage them effectively.

2. **Use Deep Breathing Techniques**

    Deep breathing is a simple yet powerful way to regulate emotions, especially in high-stress situations. When you feel overwhelmed, taking a few deep breaths can activate the body's relaxation response, slowing your heart rate and calming your mind. Try inhaling deeply for a count of four, holding for a count of four, and exhaling for a count of four. Regular practice of deep breathing can help you remain calm and grounded, even in challenging moments. Incorporate it as part of your daily routine or use it as an immediate strategy when you feel stress building.

3. Pause and Reflect Before Responding

When emotions run high, it's easy to react impulsively. Instead, train yourself to pause before responding. A few moments of reflection can provide the clarity needed to choose a constructive response rather than an emotional reaction. The next time you receive critical feedback or encounter a stressful situation, try this sequence:

1. Take a deep breath.
2. Mentally step back from the situation.
3. Ask yourself: "What response would be most helpful in this moment?"

By building in this brief pause, you allow your rational mind to take the lead, reducing the likelihood of reacting in ways that may escalate the situation.

4. Reframe Your Thoughts

Our thoughts significantly influence our emotions. When you face a challenging situation, try reframing your perspective to reduce stress and maintain a balanced outlook. For example, if a project faces unexpected challenges, instead of thinking, "This is a disaster," try reframing it as, "This is a chance to practice resilience and problem-solving."

Reframing helps you focus on growth rather than stress. By viewing challenges as opportunities for development, you can transform emotional triggers into sources of strength and learning.

MANAGING EMOTIONS: KEEPING COOL UNDER PRESSURE

The pressure to perform, make tough decisions, and project confidence can leave leaders feeling like they have no one to turn to when they need help. This isolation can lead to burnout, stress, and poor decision-making. That's why developing a robust support network is essential. Surrounding yourself with trusted colleagues, mentors, or friends provides a safe, non-judgmental space to express your feelings, share your struggles, and gain perspective. When you invite others into your leadership journey, you create a circle of encouragement, guidance, and shared wisdom. Here are several practical ways to build a support network, along with examples:

5. Build a Support Network

Leadership can often feel isolating, especially when the success of your team and organization rests heavily on your shoulders. The pressure to always perform, make tough decisions, and project confidence can create a sense of loneliness. That's why building a strong support network is crucial. Surrounding yourself with trusted mentors, peers, and friends provides a safe space to share your struggles, gain perspective, and receive guidance. These relationships offer encouragement during difficult times and remind you that you are not alone in your leadership journey. Practical Ways to Build a Support Network:

Seek Out Mentors Identify experienced leaders you respect—those who have walked the leadership path before you. Mentors offer valuable wisdom, challenge your thinking, and provide reassurance when you face difficult choices.

- *Example:* A retired school superintendent can offer insights specific to educational leadership. Regular coffee meetings or phone check-ins can provide ongoing guidance.
- *How to Start:* Reach out with a simple message like, "I admire your work as a leader. Would you be open to meeting occasionally so I can learn from your experience?"

Form a Peer Leadership Group Build a small group of leaders from similar or diverse fields who meet regularly to exchange ideas and support one another. These gatherings create a sounding board where you can share challenges, celebrate successes, and receive honest feedback.

- *Example:* A monthly breakfast with principals from neighboring school districts can foster camaraderie and idea-sharing.
- *How to Start:* Contact a few peers and suggest an informal monthly meeting over coffee or lunch. Let the group evolve naturally over time.

Join Professional Networks or Associations Engage with professional organizations that connect you to others facing similar leadership challenges. These groups often host workshops, conferences, and online forums that foster lasting connections.

- *Example:* Joining the National Association of Elementary School Principals (NAESP) can introduce you to a network of supportive leaders across the country. Conferences often spark relationships that extend beyond the event.
- *How to Start:* Become an active participant in a professional organization. Introduce yourself at events, exchange contact information, and stay engaged after meetings.

Leverage Online Communities Virtual platforms like LinkedIn, Facebook leadership groups, and professional forums can expand your support network, especially when geographic barriers exist. These communities provide real-time advice, diverse perspectives, and opportunities to learn from others.

- *Example:* A Facebook group for educational leaders can offer quick advice when you're facing a pressing issue.
- *How to Start:* Join groups relevant to your leadership role. Begin by engaging with others' posts before gradually sharing your own experiences and questions.

Nurture Trusted Friendships Not all support needs to be professional. Relationships with friends outside your leadership role can offer emotional relief and perspective beyond work. Sometimes, you simply need someone to remind you that you are more than your job title.

- *Example:* A lifelong friend in an unrelated field can offer fresh insights or simply listen without judgment.
- *How to Start:* Prioritize regular check-ins or casual gatherings. Focus on connection rather than work-related discussions.

Embrace Vulnerability Strong networks are built on trust and authenticity. Leaders often feel pressure to project strength, but real connections come from being honest about struggles. Vulnerability invites others to share their own challenges, creating mutual support.

- *Example:* Admitting to a colleague that you're feeling overwhelmed can lead to discovering they've faced similar issues—and they may offer helpful coping strategies.
- *How to Start:* Take small steps toward vulnerability. Start a conversation with, "I've been struggling with this—have you experienced something similar?"

The Benefits of a Strong Support Network:

- **Reduces Isolation:** Reminds you that others share similar challenges.

- **Provides Diverse Perspectives:** Helps you see solutions from different viewpoints.
- **Strengthens Resilience:** Reinforces your confidence when facing adversity.
- **Improves Decision-Making:** Allows you to gather trusted feedback before making key choices.
- **Encourages Growth:** Surrounding yourself with supportive individuals challenges you to develop both personally and professionally.

Leadership was never meant to be a solo journey. A support network becomes your anchor in difficult seasons and your cheering section when you succeed. Be intentional about building these relationships—they will become one of your greatest assets as a leader.

6. Practice Regular Self-Care

Emotional regulation is challenging when you're physically or mentally exhausted. Prioritizing self-care—through sleep, exercise, healthy eating, and relaxation activities—helps you maintain the resilience needed to manage emotions effectively. When you take care of your own well-being, you're better equipped to show up fully for your team.

Leadership demands can often blur the line between work and personal life, leaving little time to recharge. However, sustainable leadership requires intentional rest and balance. Taking care of yourself is not a sign of weakness—it's a strategic investment in your well-being and long-term effectiveness.

Schedule regular breaks throughout your day. Stepping away, even for a few minutes, helps reset your mind and prevents burnout. Short breaks can be as simple as a five-minute walk, a breathing exercise, or enjoying a quiet moment with a cup of coffee. These pauses improve focus, creativity, and decision-making.

Set boundaries around work hours. Resist the urge to always be "on." Clearly define when your workday begins and ends—and honor those boundaries. Turn off notifications after hours, avoid checking emails late at night, and give yourself permission to unplug. Protecting your time helps prevent work from overtaking every aspect of your life.

Engage in activities that refuel you. Leadership is emotionally and mentally taxing, so regularly invest in activities that restore your energy. This could mean exercising, pursuing a hobby, spending time with loved ones, reading, or simply getting outside in nature. These moments of joy and connection are not distractions from leadership—they strengthen your capacity to lead well.

Calendar what you care about. If something matters, put it on your schedule. Treat rest, exercise, family time, and hobbies with the same importance as meetings and deadlines. When you prioritize self-care on your calendar, it becomes a non-negotiable part of your day. Protect these commitments like you would any critical work task.

Ultimately, self-care is not a luxury—it's essential for effective, enduring leadership. A rested, healthy leader is far better equipped to inspire, problem-solve, and lead with clarity.

7. Use Visualization for Calmness and Clarity

Visualization is a powerful tool that can help you prepare for high-stakes situations by mentally rehearsing how you'll respond. Before a challenging meeting or presentation, take a few moments to visualize yourself handling the situation calmly and confidently. Imagine how you want to feel, the words you want to use, and the tone you want to convey. Visualization helps you mentally prepare for stressful moments, making it easier to stay composed and focused. By envisioning your ideal response, you reinforce positive behavior and enhance your confidence.

Modeling Emotional Stability for Your Team

Leaders set the tone for their teams, especially in high-stress situations. When you remain calm, focused, and optimistic, you create a sense of stability that helps others feel secure. Here are some ways to model emotional stability for your team:

1. **Be Transparent but Reassuring**

    Transparency fosters trust, especially during challenging times. If your team is facing uncertainty, be honest about the situation but also emphasize the steps being taken to address it. A calm, reassuring tone shows that you're handling the situation and that you have faith in your team's ability to work through it together.

2. **Encourage a Positive Problem-Solving Approach**

    When issues arise, encourage your team to view them as opportunities for growth rather than setbacks. Model a problem-solving approach that focuses on solutions rather than dwelling on difficulties. This perspective reinforces the idea that challenges are normal and manageable parts of the work.

3. **Show Empathy and Understanding**

    Acknowledge the emotions and challenges your team may be experiencing. Empathy builds connection and reinforces that you care about their well-being. Showing understanding doesn't mean absorbing others' stress but rather offering a supportive presence that fosters resilience and optimism. For example, if a project deadline is causing stress, acknowledge the pressure and offer support. Saying something like, "I know this is a challenging time, and I appreciate your hard work. Let's discuss how we can support each other to meet this goal," helps create a collaborative, supportive environment.

Conclusion: Leading with Emotional Intelligence

Mastering emotional regulation is a powerful skill that allows you to lead with confidence, resilience, and empathy. By managing your emotions effectively, you create a stable foundation for yourself and your team, fostering a culture where everyone can approach challenges with clarity and focus. Emotions are a natural part of the human experience, and learning to navigate them constructively strengthens your ability to connect, inspire, and guide those around you.

As you continue your leadership journey, remember that emotional resilience is built over time through self-awareness, practice, and intentionality. Each stressful situation provides an opportunity to refine your responses and reinforce your commitment to growth. By cultivating emotional stability, you empower your team to face challenges with a calm, focused mindset, making it easier for everyone to thrive.

While mastering emotional regulation is essential, there are deeper, more insidious challenges that often undermine leaders from within: insecurity and self-doubt. These "silent saboteurs" can erode your confidence, influence your decisions, and hold you back from reaching your full potential. In the next chapter, we'll explore how these internal doubts can subtly undermine leadership effectiveness, and we'll discuss practical strategies for recognizing, confronting, and overcoming them.

Chapter Seven will guide you through understanding the sources of self-doubt and insecurity, how they manifest in your leadership, and the ways to build a resilient mindset that allows you to lead with authentic confidence. By addressing these silent challenges, you'll strengthen your foundation as a leader and unlock new levels of self-assurance, adaptability, and fulfillment in your role.

Self-Reflection Prompt

Reflect on a recent situation where you felt emotionally triggered or under significant pressure as a leader. Consider how you responded in the moment and how it may have impacted your interactions with others and the overall outcome. Take note of any recurring patterns in your emotional responses to challenging situations.

Reflection Question

What emotions tend to surface when you're under pressure, and how do they affect your behavior as a leader? In what ways might managing these emotions differently improve your effectiveness and the environment for your team? Take time to jot down your thoughts, and consider one or two strategies you could practice to maintain calmness in future high-stress situations. These reflections can guide you toward developing greater emotional resilience and fostering a more composed, supportive leadership presence.

MANAGING EMOTIONS: KEEPING COOL UNDER PRESSURE

LESSONS LEARNED

DeAndre had always considered himself a steady leader. As superintendent of Maple Creek Schools, he'd navigated budget cuts, new mandates, and tense negotiations with relative ease. But the announcement that the district's largest elementary school would need extensive renovations after an unexpected facilities inspection shook even his calm demeanor.

Teachers were understandably nervous—classrooms would have to be relocated, schedules adjusted, and some routines disrupted. Parents were anxious about safety and the impact on learning. Community members worried about costs and timelines. Everywhere DeAndre turned, he faced concerned faces, pointed questions, and more demands than he had immediate answers for.

The first public forum on the matter was scheduled for a Thursday evening in the high school auditorium. In the days leading up to it, DeAndre's stress mounted. He'd never felt so on edge. His stomach twisted at the thought of standing before hundreds of parents and staff, many of whom felt upset or fearful. The old DeAndre might have tried to power through his anxiety by preparing lengthy statements, rehearsing every possible answer, and steeling himself with a curt, businesslike demeanor. But he recalled the insights from Chapter Six—about acknowledging emotions, understanding their root causes, and responding thoughtfully rather than reacting impulsively.

On the afternoon of the forum, DeAndre took a moment alone in his office. He admitted to himself: *I'm nervous. I'm worried I won't have perfect answers. I'm afraid of looking unprepared and losing their trust.* He let those feelings come, without judgment. Then he took a few deep breaths, focusing on inhaling slowly and exhaling fully. After a moment, he asked himself the questions he'd learned to use: *What do these feelings tell me?* They told him that this situation mattered deeply, that he cared about the well-being of the students, teachers, and families. *How can I respond in a way that aligns with my values?* He valued honesty, empathy, and stability. He decided to lead with openness, acknowledging uncertainties but promising collaborative problem-solving.

When DeAndre stepped onto the stage that night, he carried his emotions not as a burden but as information. He looked out at the sea of worried faces and began by expressing gratitude for their attendance and their genuine concern. Instead of offering pat reassurances, he acknowledged the difficulties: "I understand the anxiety this situation creates. I know many of you have questions we can't fully answer yet, and that's unsettling. Here's what I can tell you: we are committed to student safety, quality instruction, and keeping you informed every step of the way."

A parent's voice trembled as she asked about where her son's class would meet if classrooms were off-limits. Another teacher demanded specifics on how materials would be moved. In the past, the intensity might have rattled DeAndre, pushing him to snap into defensive mode. Now, he listened calmly, steadying himself with each breath. He didn't pretend to have all the details at that very moment, but he offered a timeline for updates and invited staff members to join a task force to shape solutions. He empathized with their frustrations: "I know this is hard. We're facing this challenge together, and I need your input to find the best path forward."

As the evening progressed, something shifted in the room. Although not everyone left satisfied—they still wanted clearer answers—most people expressed appreciation for DeAndre's demeanor. They noted that he was neither dismissive nor evasive. He didn't let emotional tension drive him to over-promise or react harshly. Instead, his calm, measured approach signaled that while the road ahead might be bumpy, they had a leader who would guide them without panicking.

Over the following weeks, DeAndre continued to apply these emotional management strategies. In meetings with principals, he acknowledged the stress they faced and encouraged them to share concerns openly. When teachers voiced worries, he listene

MANAGING EMOTIONS: KEEPING COOL UNDER PRESSURE

> attentively and responded thoughtfully, rather than rushing to put a positive spin on everything. He was honest about uncertainties and complexities, and he worked collaboratively to navigate them.
>
> By modeling emotional regulation, DeAndre set a tone for the district. Principals noticed how his calm approach diffused tension in their own schools. Teachers felt more at ease, even if the solutions were still in progress. Parents, seeing their superintendent's steadiness, believed that though the challenge was real, it would be handled with care and competence.
>
> In this way, the lessons from Chapter Six came to life. By understanding his emotions, responding with intention rather than impulse, and leading with steady composure, DeAndre turned a potential crisis into an opportunity to build trust and show the true strength of his leadership.

CHAPTER SEVEN

The Silent Saboteurs: Addressing Insecurity and Self-Doubt

Leadership can often feel like walking a tightrope. While leaders are expected to project confidence, clarity, and decisiveness, it's common to grapple internally with insecurities and self-doubt. These "silent saboteurs" can be especially insidious because they work quietly, undermining confidence and clouding decision-making from within. Unlike external challenges, which are easier to see and confront, self-doubt and insecurity can be deeply ingrained, often lying beneath the surface and influencing our behaviors in subtle but powerful ways.

This chapter explores how internal doubts can impact leadership and why addressing them is essential to becoming a more resilient, authentic, and effective leader. We'll delve into the sources of insecurity, common ways it manifests, and practical strategies for confronting self-doubt head-on. By learning to recognize and manage these silent saboteurs, you can break free from their influence, develop greater self-assurance, and empower yourself to lead with genuine confidence.

Why Insecurity and Self-Doubt Undermine Leadership

Insecurity and self-doubt aren't inherently harmful; in small doses, they can keep us humble, open to learning, and grounded. However, when left unchecked, they become barriers to effective leadership. Here's why addressing them is essential:

1. **They Distort Decision-Making**
   When insecurity creeps in, it can distort our judgment, making us second-guess our decisions or overly rely on others for validation. This hesitation can lead to indecisiveness, delays, and a lack of clear direction, which can frustrate your team and erode their confidence in your leadership.

2. **They Create a Need for Validation**
   Insecure leaders may become overly reliant on external approval, constantly seeking validation to reassure themselves of their worth. This need can lead to micromanagement, overworking, or people-pleasing behaviors that compromise integrity, dilute authority, and hinder authentic leadership.

3. **They Damage Relationships and Trust**
   When leaders are driven by insecurity, they may react defensively to feedback, avoid difficult conversations, or fail to acknowledge mistakes. This behavior makes it difficult for team members to trust and connect with them, eroding the open, trusting relationships essential for effective teamwork.

4. **They Limit Growth and Risk-Taking**
   Insecurity often makes leaders avoid risks and play it safe to prevent potential criticism or failure. This fear of failure stifles innovation

and limits the leader's growth and the team's potential. By playing it safe, insecure leaders may end up missing out on valuable learning experiences and bold opportunities for progress.

Common Sources of Insecurity and Self-Doubt in Leadership

Understanding the roots of self-doubt is the first step toward addressing it. While each person's experience is unique, here are some common sources of insecurity and self-doubt among leaders:

1. **Comparison with Others**

    Many leaders fall into the trap of measuring their worth against others—whether it's a colleague who appears to excel effortlessly or a mentor whose achievements seem out of reach. Social media and professional networks can amplify this comparison, presenting curated versions of others' successes without revealing their struggles. This habit can distort reality, leading you to fixate on others' strengths while minimizing your own.

    Comparison can be particularly dangerous because it shifts your focus outward instead of inward. Rather than developing your unique leadership style, you may start mimicking others or feeling like you'll never measure up. True growth happens when you focus on your progress, strengths, and values, understanding that every leader's path is different.

Practical Shift: When you notice yourself comparing, pause and ask:

- *What can I learn from this person?*
- *What strengths do I bring to my leadership role?*
- *How have I grown over the past year?*

Shifting from comparison to curiosity and self-reflection helps reframe others' success as inspiration rather than competition.

2. **Imposter Syndrome**

Imposter syndrome—the belief that you are not truly qualified for your role—can plague even the most accomplished leaders. You may attribute your achievements to luck, timing, or the contributions of others, while secretly fearing that you will be "exposed" as incompetent.

This internal narrative often drives behaviors like perfectionism, over-preparation, or avoiding opportunities that might reveal your perceived weaknesses. Leaders with imposter syndrome may struggle to accept praise, feeling like they haven't truly earned it.

Over my 23-year career as a school leader, I have personally grappled with imposter syndrome. Despite outward accomplishments—leading successful initiatives, seeing students thrive, and building a strong school culture—I often questioned my capabilities. I would wonder, *Am I truly making the right decisions? Do I have what it takes to lead this community?* These thoughts sometimes led me to second-guess my choices or work tirelessly to prove my worth.

However, through mentorship, self-reflection, and leaning into my faith and values, I've come to realize that self-doubt doesn't disqualify you—it makes you human. Those moments of questioning have kept me humble and driven me to learn, adapt, and lead with empathy.

Practical Shift:

- Normalize the feeling—remind yourself that many successful leaders experience imposter syndrome.
- Keep a "wins folder"—document positive feedback, successful outcomes, and affirmations from colleagues to revisit when doubt creeps in.

- Seek feedback—trusted mentors and colleagues can provide a reality check, affirming your strengths and helping you see your blind spots.

3. Past Failures and Criticism

Failures and harsh feedback have a way of embedding themselves deeply in our minds, often louder than our successes. As leaders, we can replay these moments—an initiative that didn't work out, a tough performance review, or a public mistake—allowing them to shape our confidence moving forward.

These experiences can create a fear of risk-taking or cause you to hesitate when making bold decisions. You may start leading defensively, focusing more on avoiding mistakes than pursuing innovation. However, failure is an essential part of leadership growth. The most effective leaders are those who embrace setbacks as learning opportunities, using them to refine their approach and strengthen their resilience.

Practical Shift:

- Reframe failures as lessons. Ask: *What did this teach me? How has it made me a better leader?*
- Separate your identity from your performance. A failed project does not mean you are a failed leader.
- Regularly reflect on both your successes and challenges, recognizing how both have shaped your leadership journey.

4. Internalized Expectations and Perfectionism

Many leaders carry the weight of their own sky-high expectations—believing they must always have the answers, be strong for their team, and achieve flawless results. This perfectionistic mindset can lead to chronic stress, burnout, and the inability to appreciate progress.

Perfectionism often masks underlying self-doubt. It creates an "all-or-nothing" mentality—anything less than perfect feels like failure. Leaders caught in this cycle may struggle to delegate, fearing that others won't meet their standards, or they may delay decisions out of fear of getting it wrong. Yet, leadership is not about perfection—it's about progress, adaptability, and authenticity. Teams respect leaders who admit mistakes and model growth more than those who appear infallible.

> Leadership is not about perfection—it's about progress, adaptability, and authenticity.

Practical Shift:

- Set realistic standards. Ask yourself: *Would I expect this level of perfection from someone else?*
- Celebrate small wins and progress, not just end results.
- Remind yourself: Excellence is the goal—not perfection.

5. External Pressure and High Expectations

Leadership carries the weight of visibility. Team members look to you for stability, stakeholders demand results, and communities expect you to inspire and lead with confidence. This constant external pressure can make you feel like every decision you make is scrutinized under a microscope, increasing your fear of falling short.

The desire to meet everyone's expectations can lead to people-pleasing, overcommitting, or suppressing your own ideas to avoid conflict. This can erode your confidence and authenticity over time. However, effective leadership requires discerning whose voices matter most. You cannot please everyone, but you can lead with integrity, transparency, and a clear sense of purpose.

THE SILENT SABOTEURS: ADDRESSING INSECURITY AND SELF-DOUBT

Practical Shift:

- Clarify your core values—let them guide your decisions when pressure mounts.
- Communicate openly with stakeholders. Set realistic expectations and involve others in solutions.
- Accept that leadership will involve criticism. Growth often happens when you stand firm in your convictions, even when others disagree.

Self-doubt and insecurity are not signs of poor leadership—they are part of the leadership journey. They remind us that we care deeply about our work and the people we serve. The key is not to eliminate these feelings but to learn how to navigate them with resilience, self-awareness, and support. Over time, you'll discover that your imperfections are not barriers to leadership—they are what make you a more empathetic, adaptable, and authentic leader.

> **Self-doubt and insecurity are not signs of poor leadership—they are part of the leadership journey.**

Recognizing the Signs of Insecurity in Leadership

Insecurity can manifest in various ways, often subtly. Here are some common signs that self-doubt may be impacting your leadership:

- Overanalyzing decisions and constantly second-guessing yourself
- Seeking excessive reassurance or approval from others

- Avoiding responsibility or downplaying achievements
- Reacting defensively to constructive feedback
- Struggling to delegate or micromanaging tasks
- Feeling like an "imposter" despite your accomplishments
- Playing it safe and avoiding risks to minimize criticism

Recognizing these behaviors is essential to confronting insecurity. They can be subtle at first, but when you start to notice these patterns, you can begin addressing the root causes of your self-doubt.

Strategies for Overcoming Insecurity and Building Self-Confidence

Overcoming insecurity and self-doubt is a process that involves self-awareness, self-compassion, and intentional action. Here are several strategies to help you confront these silent saboteurs and strengthen your confidence as a leader:

1. **Identify and Challenge Negative Self-Talk**

    Negative self-talk is a common source of self-doubt. Thoughts like "I'm not good enough" or "I'll never be as skilled as others" can quickly spiral, undermining your confidence. Start by identifying these thoughts and challenging their validity. Ask yourself if they're based on evidence or if they're distortions rooted in fear.

    Try replacing negative self-talk with constructive affirmations. For example, instead of "I'm not qualified for this role," try reframing it as "I'm committed to learning and growing in this role." Shifting your internal dialogue can help you break free from limiting beliefs and reinforce a more positive self-image.

    Negative self-talk often stems from the "stories" we tell ourselves—interpretations and assumptions about events that may not be entirely factual. In Crucial Conversations, the authors emphasize the importance of separating facts from stories to navigate challenging emotions effectively. When faced with negative self-talk, the first step is to pause and identify the raw facts of the situation, stripping away the narrative we've constructed. For example, instead of saying, "I'm a terrible leader because someone disagreed with me," focus on the fact that a disagreement occurred. Next, challenge the story by asking yourself: "What evidence do I have? Could there be another perspective?" This process encourages a shift from self-criticism to curiosity and objectivity. Finally, replace the negative story with a more constructive one, rooted in self-compassion and growth. By approaching negative self-talk in this way, we can gain clarity, reduce emotional reactivity, and foster healthier, more productive self-dialogues.

2. **Embrace Self-Compassion**

Many leaders hold themselves to a higher standard than they would anyone else. If you wouldn't harshly judge a team member for a mistake, why would you do it to yourself? Self-compassion means treating yourself with kindness, understanding that everyone makes mistakes, and recognizing that you're doing your best.

When insecurity surfaces, practice self-compassion by acknowledging your feelings without judgment. For example, if you're feeling inadequate after a difficult meeting, remind yourself that it's normal to have off days and that you can learn and grow from the experience. Self-compassion is not about lowering standards but rather about giving yourself grace as you strive to meet them.

3. **Reflect on Past Successes**

Insecure leaders often forget to acknowledge their own accomplishments, focusing only on perceived shortcomings. Take time to reflect on past successes and the positive impact you've had on your team, school, or organization. Recalling specific instances when you made a difference can help reinforce your abilities and remind you of the skills that brought you to your current position.

Consider keeping a "success journal" where you document achievements, positive feedback, and milestones. Revisiting this journal during moments of self-doubt can provide a tangible reminder of your capabilities and accomplishments.

4. Accept That Failure Is Part of Growth

Insecurity often stems from a fear of failure. By shifting your perspective on failure—from something to be avoided at all costs to a natural part of learning—you can reduce the power it holds over you. Failure doesn't define your worth; it's an opportunity to learn, grow, and improve.

When you encounter setbacks, approach them as learning experiences. Ask yourself: "What can I learn from this? How can I use this experience to grow?" This growth-oriented mindset will allow you to view challenges and mistakes as valuable steppingstones on your leadership journey.

5. Seek Feedback as a Tool for Growth

Constructive feedback is essential for growth, but it can be intimidating for leaders struggling with self-doubt. Instead of viewing feedback as a critique, see it as an opportunity to learn and improve. Cultivating an open attitude toward feedback helps you build resilience and address areas of insecurity proactively.

Invite feedback from trusted colleagues or mentors who can offer honest, supportive insights. Consider asking questions like, "What's one area where I could improve?" or "How can I better support our team?" This approach not only provides valuable information but also reinforces your commitment to growth.

6. **Focus on Your Strengths and Unique Qualities**

   Everyone brings unique qualities to leadership. Rather than comparing yourself to others, focus on the strengths and skills that make you effective. Embrace the qualities that set you apart, and find ways to leverage them in your work.

   For instance, if you're a great listener, emphasize that skill when working with your team. If you excel at strategic planning, lean into that strength when setting goals. By recognizing your unique strengths, you'll develop a more secure sense of identity and feel less inclined to compare yourself to others.

Conclusion: Embracing Confidence Through Self-Acceptance

Addressing insecurity and self-doubt isn't about becoming an infallible leader; it's about embracing your whole self—strengths, limitations, and all. By learning to manage these silent saboteurs, you free yourself to lead with a balanced sense of confidence grounded in authenticity. True confidence doesn't come from denying your insecurities but from accepting them, working through them, and growing as a result.

As you confront your internal doubts and insecurities, you'll find that they lose their hold over you. In their place, you'll develop a resilient, self-assured mindset that allows you to face challenges with grace, take risks without fear, and make decisions with clarity. By leading from a place of self-acceptance, you create a foundation of strength that empowers you to inspire, support, and guide others with genuine confidence.

With a foundation of self-acceptance, the next step toward authentic leadership is embracing transparency. In the next chapter, we'll explore how acknowledging and sharing your limitations openly can build trust, foster connection, and create a culture of openness. By leading with honesty and vulnerability, you invite your team to bring their full selves to the work, creating an environment where everyone feels valued and understood.

Chapter Eight will guide you through strategies for integrating transparency into your leadership style, helping you to turn weaknesses into opportunities for building trust and strengthening team dynamics. Embracing transparency allows you to lead not from a place of perfection but from a place of authenticity, inspiring those around you to do the same.

Ready to Meet Your Inner Critic?

Before you move on, take a few moments to complete the Self-Saboteur Self-Assessment on the next page. This short, reflective tool is designed to help you identify the ways insecurity and self-doubt may be showing up in your leadership. Be honest with yourself, there are no wrong answers here. Use your results as a starting point for deeper reflection, and consider revisiting them over time as your self-awareness grows. Let's see what your *inner saboteur* has to say and how you can start rewriting their script.

Self-Saboteur Self-Assessment

Answer each question with the number that best represents your typical response:

1. I compare myself to other leaders and often feel like I don't measure up.
    - o   1 (Rarely)
    - o   2 (Sometimes)
    - o   3 (Frequently)
    - o   4 (Constantly)

2. When I receive constructive feedback, my first reaction is to feel defensive or discouraged.
   - o   1 (Not at all)
   - o   2 (A little bit)
   - o   3 (Quite a bit)
   - o   4 (A lot)
3. I often feel like I need to double-check my decisions with others to feel confident.
   - o   1 (Almost never)
   - o   2 (Occasionally)
   - o   3 (Quite often)
   - o   4 (Constantly)
4. I avoid taking risks because I'm afraid of failing or being judged.
   - o   1 (Nope, I'm bold!)
   - o   2 (Once in a while)
   - o   3 (Frequently)
   - o   4 (Regularly)
5. I struggle to celebrate my achievements because I think they don't really count or that anyone could have accomplished them.
   - o   1 (I'm proud of my wins!)
   - o   2 (I'm humble but proud)
   - o   3 (It's hard for me)
   - o   4 (I brush off my successes)
6. I feel like I have to constantly prove myself to others.
   - o   1 (Not really)
   - o   2 (Sometimes)
   - o   3 (Yes, often)
   - o   4 (Absolutely, always)

7. When faced with a new challenge, I immediately wonder if I'm capable enough to handle it.
    o   1 (I dive right in!)
    o   2 (I have a few doubts but still go for it)
    o   3 (I hesitate)
    o   4 (I'm paralyzed by uncertainty)
8. I replay past mistakes in my mind, fearing they might repeat.
    o   1 (I've moved on)
    o   2 (They occasionally pop up)
    o   3 (They weigh on me)
    o   4 (I obsess over them)

Scoring
Total your scores and find your self-saboteur personality below:

8–12: The Self-Assured Super Star
You've mastered the art of confidence, and self-doubt rarely sneaks into your leadership. You have an admirable resilience, with a healthy balance of humility and confidence. Keep inspiring others with your grounded, self-assured leadership.

13–18: The Humble Hero
You occasionally let doubt visit, but you don't let it move in. You're aware of your insecurities but manage them well, often using them as a chance for growth. Stay vigilant and keep fostering your strengths—just don't be afraid to celebrate your wins now and then!

19–24: The Cautious Commander
Self-doubt often taps you on the shoulder, and you might be playing it a bit too safe. You're mindful of your decisions, but sometimes that mindfulness holds you back. Practice embracing mistakes as learning opportunities, and try to step outside your comfort zone in small ways.

25–32: *The Overthinking Overlord*

You may be letting self-doubt and insecurity sabotage your leadership more than you realize. It's time to start tackling these saboteurs head-on. Acknowledge your strengths, set boundaries on overthinking, and remember that you don't have to prove yourself to anyone but yourself. Practice self-compassion, and consider seeking feedback to ground your perspective.

CHAPTER EIGHT

Visible Leadership: Leading Authentically in the Face of Adversity

For many leaders, the idea of being vulnerable or showing weakness is uncomfortable, even frightening. Leadership is often associated with strength, composure, and the ability to rise above challenges. But real leadership doesn't mean pretending to be invincible. In fact, some of the most powerful and lasting leadership moments come from a place of honesty and openness—including those times when we admit our limitations.

Transparency in leadership isn't just about sharing successes; it's about embracing moments of uncertainty and admitting when we don't have all the answers. When leaders model this kind of honesty, it fosters trust and connection, creating a culture in which team members feel safe to be themselves and share their own struggles. This chapter will explore the power of leading authentically through weakness and offer insights on how embracing transparency can transform not only your leadership but the very fabric of your team. Let's start with a story of a leader who dared to show his vulnerability and the impact it had on those he led.

A Story of Leading Through Openly and Authentically

In a small school district, Principal Mark Dalton was known for his energy, organization, and relentless dedication to his staff and students. He was the kind of leader who always seemed to have everything under control. His team admired him, not only because he was efficient and thoughtful, but because he genuinely cared about his school and the community it served.

But one year, everything changed. Mark's wife was diagnosed with a serious illness, and suddenly, his world shifted. He found himself juggling countless hospital visits, long hours, and the overwhelming anxiety that comes with watching a loved one suffer. Despite this, he felt obligated to keep everything at work running smoothly, to maintain his image as the leader who could "handle it all."

For a while, he managed to do just that. But as the months went on, the weight of his responsibilities at home and at school began to wear on him. His usual enthusiasm waned, and small mistakes started slipping into his work. Teachers began to notice his absence at meetings and his distracted responses when they sought guidance. They, too, began to feel the impact. Tensions were rising, and without realizing it, Mark was pulling back from the people who depended on him.

Finally, one morning after a particularly long night at the hospital, Mark arrived late to a staff meeting. He looked tired, worn, and unlike his usual self. As he stood at the front of the room, he felt the familiar urge to put on his "strong face" and assure everyone that things were fine. But he couldn't. Looking around the room, seeing the concerned faces of his team, he felt the weight of it all overwhelm him. For the first time, Mark found himself in tears in front of his staff. He apologized for his lateness and, in a wavering voice, explained the situation with his wife, the sleepless nights, and the struggle he had been trying so hard to keep to himself.

In that moment, something extraordinary happened. His staff didn't see him as a leader who was faltering; they saw him as a human being, someone they could relate to, someone who trusted them enough to share his pain. After he finished speaking, one teacher stood up and hugged him. Then another. Soon, the room was filled with comforting voices, assuring him that they would support him however he needed.

From that day forward, something shifted within the school. Teachers who had previously been hesitant to ask for help now felt more comfortable reaching out to each other, knowing that even their leader needed support sometimes. Mark's honesty not only deepened the trust within his team but inspired others to bring their full selves to work. They became more willing to share their own struggles, offer each other help, and create a school environment that was more connected, compassionate, and resilient.

The Power of Vulnerability in Leadership

Mark's story illustrates an essential truth about leadership: vulnerability and transparency are not signs of weakness; they are foundations of strength. When leaders acknowledge their struggles and allow themselves to be seen as whole, imperfect people, they create an atmosphere of authenticity that empowers everyone to be more open and honest. Here are some of the powerful effects of embracing transparency in leadership:

1. **Build Trust Through Authentic Leadership**

    Trust is the foundation of every successful team, and it starts with a leader's willingness to be transparent and authentic. When leaders are open about their thoughts, challenges, and even uncertainties, it signals to their teams that they are genuine and trustworthy. People respect and connect with leaders who are real—not those who pretend to have all the answers.

Transparency doesn't mean oversharing every detail; it means being honest about your decision-making processes, admitting when you're unsure, and communicating openly—even when the news is difficult. When team members see this level of honesty, it fosters a sense of psychological safety. They know they won't be blindsided, manipulated, or left guessing about important matters.

Key Impact:

- Teams feel secure and respected, which encourages loyalty and engagement.
- Leaders earn credibility, because honesty builds long-term trust—even during tough times.
- Employees are more likely to approach leaders with concerns, knowing they will receive honesty in return.

Practical Steps:

- Communicate openly about challenges and the rationale behind decisions.
- Admit when you don't know something and invite others to help find solutions.
- Follow through on commitments—consistency reinforces trust.

2. Cultivating Empathy, Connection, and Psychological Safety

When leaders lead with transparency and vulnerability, it breaks down the walls of hierarchy and reminds everyone that they are part of the same human experience. Sharing personal challenges—whether it's balancing work and family, dealing with uncertainty, or navigating a difficult project—shows that leaders face struggles, too. This fosters empathy and emotional connection within the team.

A leader's vulnerability creates permission for others to bring their whole selves to work. Team members begin to feel safe admitting when they are overwhelmed, asking for help, or offering honest feedback. Over time, this sense of psychological safety leads to stronger relationships, better teamwork, and a healthier work environment.

Key Impact:

- Employees feel valued as people, not just as workers.
- Teams develop mutual respect, leading to better collaboration.
- Emotional support becomes a cultural norm, reducing stress and burnout.

Practical Steps:

- Regularly check in on team members' well-being—not just their work progress.
- Model empathy by listening attentively and acknowledging emotions during discussions.
- Share personal experiences when appropriate to normalize vulnerability.

3. Unlocking Creativity and Inspiring Authentic Contribution

A transparent and authentic leader fosters an environment in which innovation can thrive. When people know their ideas will be heard and that mistakes won't lead to adverse consequences, they feel emboldened to think creatively and take calculated risks. Leaders who openly discuss their own failures and lessons learned demonstrate that imperfection is not only accepted, but valued.

Authenticity also sets the tone for the entire team. When leaders show up as their true selves—acknowledging both their strengths and weaknesses—they empower others to do the same. This unlocks each person's potential, encouraging diverse perspectives and original thinking. In this kind of environment, individuals are more likely to voice bold ideas, challenge the status quo, and contribute fully.

Key Impact:

- Teams feel free to innovate without fear of failure.
- Diverse ideas surface because people know their input is valued.
- Authenticity becomes a cultural norm, strengthening team morale.

Practical Steps:

- Celebrate creative attempts—even those that don't succeed—to reinforce that risk-taking is valued.
- Encourage open brainstorming sessions where "bad ideas" are welcomed as steppingstones.
- Share your own learning experiences to demonstrate that growth comes from both success and failure.

Transparent, authentic leadership is not about being perfect—it's about being real. When leaders embrace honesty, vulnerability, and openness, they create an environment where trust flourishes, teams connect on a deeper level, and creativity becomes a natural outcome.

> **Transparent, authentic leadership is not about being perfect—it's about being real.**

This type of culture doesn't just drive performance—it nurtures people, allowing both leaders and teams to thrive together.

How to Lead Authentically in the Face of Adversity

Leading during times of adversity requires courage, self-awareness, and a willingness to be vulnerable. Here are several strategies to help you embrace transparency and build a culture of trust within your team:

1. **Acknowledge Your Humanity**

    One of the most powerful things a leader can do is to acknowledge their humanity. This means admitting when you're struggling, asking for help when you need it, and letting go of the expectation that you must always appear strong. Remember, your team doesn't expect you to be perfect; they expect you to be real.

    Early in my career as a school leader, I believed I had to have all the answers, always make the right decisions, and be a pillar of strength for staff, students, and the overall community. One particular moment stands out when a tough situation brought me to my breaking point: a decision that impacted several families didn't go as planned, and I was subjected to a good deal of criticism. My instinct was to defend myself and push through as if nothing could phase me, but inside, I felt defeated. Instead of retreating, I chose to address the situation honestly with my team. I admitted that I didn't have all the answers and that I was struggling to navigate the complexity of the decision. To my surprise, my vulnerability opened the door for collaboration, understanding, and even support from those around me. That experience reminded me that acknowledging my humanity—my imperfections, doubts, and emotions—doesn't diminish my leadership; it strengthens it. It allows me to connect authentically and lead with humility.

    The next time you face a difficult situation, consider sharing it with your team in an honest but professional way. For example, you might say, "This decision has been challenging, and I'm still working through some uncertainties." This level of transparency invites others to share their own perspectives and support you.

2. **Share Personal Stories and Lessons**

Sharing stories of your own challenges and the lessons you've learned can be a powerful way to connect with your team. These stories humanize you and remind others that growth often comes from difficult experiences. When appropriate, share examples of times when you faced a setback or struggled with a decision, and explain how you navigated those moments.

For example, if you once struggled with a difficult decision, you might share that experience with your team and discuss what it taught you. This vulnerability shows that you're not only open about your past, but also willing to learn and grow alongside them.

3. **Create an Environment of Open Dialogue**

Transparency is not a one-way street; it's about fostering an environment in which everyone feels comfortable sharing their thoughts and challenges. Encourage open dialogue by actively seeking feedback and making space for honest conversations. Let your team know that you're open to hearing both positive and constructive feedback, and that their input is essential to your growth as a leader. Consider holding regular check-ins or team meetings where you invite everyone to discuss their challenges, ideas, and suggestions. By creating this space, you reinforce that transparency and openness are valued in your organization.

4. **Model Self-Acceptance and Self-Compassion**

Embracing transparency also means modeling self-acceptance. When leaders are open about their limitations without self-judgment, it sets a powerful example for the team. Practice self-compassion, and remind yourself that being a leader doesn't mean you have to be invulnerable. By accepting yourself fully, you create a ripple effect that encourages others to accept themselves as well.

5. Seek Support When Needed

Transparency also means knowing when to seek support from others. No one has all the answers, and seeking guidance or assistance from colleagues, mentors, or even your team shows that you value collaboration. This not only helps you make better decisions but reinforces a culture of mutual support.

The next time you feel uncertain, reach out to trusted advisors or team members. Let them know you value their input and want to work together to find a solution. This approach reinforces that everyone's perspectives are valuable and that leadership is a shared responsibility.

Conclusion: Strength in Vulnerability

Leading authentically requires immense courage, but the rewards are profound. By embracing your own humanity, sharing your challenges, and creating an environment of trust, you build a foundation of transparency and openness that resonates throughout your team. When leaders are honest about their struggles and limitations, they empower others to do the same, creating a culture where people feel seen, supported, and inspired to grow.

As you continue to lead with transparency, remember that vulnerability is not a weakness—it's a strength. When you let others see the full picture of who you are, you open doors to deeper connections, more genuine collaboration, and a resilient team that knows it can weather any storm.

Transparency in leadership is essential, but so is adaptability. In a constantly changing world, leaders must be willing to evolve to meet the needs of their teams and organizations. In the next chapter, we'll explore the importance of flexibility in leadership and the value of knowing when and how to adjust your approach.

Chapter Nine will offer insights into how to recognize when your leadership style might be holding you back, the benefits of adapting to different situations, and strategies for evolving as a leader without losing your core values. By learning to balance authenticity with adaptability, you'll be equipped to lead effectively through any change or challenge that comes your way.

Self-Reflection Prompt

Think back to a recent time when you felt the need to appear strong or to hide a struggle from your team. Consider what held you back from being transparent in that moment and how it affected both you and your team.

Reflection Question

What might have changed if you had shared your challenge openly? How could showing vulnerability and seeking support have impacted trust, connection, or problem-solving within your team? Write your thoughts, and consider how embracing transparency in future moments could create a more trusting and supportive environment for both you and those you lead.

LESSONS LEARNED

Rita had been principal of Lakeside Middle School for three years. In many ways, the school was thriving: test scores were on the rise, community partnerships were growing, and the staff was hardworking and dedicated. But beneath that polished surface, Rita carried a secret weight. She'd been struggling with burnout, staying late into the night to juggle administrative tasks, fighting to keep up with new district mandates, and always feeling that she couldn't show any cracks in her armor. She believed that admitting difficulty would somehow diminish her authority, leaving staff and families to wonder if she could handle the challenges of leadership.

As the school year reached its midpoint, Rita felt the strain even more acutely. She found herself snapping at small inconveniences—snippy replies to an assistant who asked a routine question, an impatient sigh when a teacher sought advice on a new program. She noticed teachers eyeing her warily, as if uncertain what mood she'd be in on any given day. Students picked up on it, too; she overheard one whisper to another, "The principal seems really stressed out lately."

Instead of brushing off these warning signs, Rita decided to confront the reality: she was tired, overwhelmed, and in need of help. She recalled the chapter's lessons about vulnerability and authenticity. Being transparent about her challenges could be the key to re-establishing trust and connection. It wouldn't mean complaining or offloading her burdens onto others—it would mean acknowledging her humanity and inviting her team to work with her, rather than apart from her.

That Friday morning, Rita asked for a brief session with the entire staff after dismissal. Gathered in the library's reading corner, teachers exchanged curious glances. Rita stood before them, hands clasped. For a moment, she hesitated. She'd always felt safest behind a polished speech, a confident plan. Now, she would step forward without that shield.

"I wanted to meet today because I realize I haven't been myself," she began, voice steady but earnest. "I've been under a lot of pressure—trying to meet new district expectations, support everyone's needs, and keep up with constant changes. I know that lately, I've been distant and short-tempered. I'm sorry. I want you all to know that I respect and value your work more than I can say, and if I've made you feel otherwise, that's on me."

An uneasy silence followed, but she pressed on. "I don't have all the answers. Sometimes, I'm unsure how to balance everything on my plate. But I believe in this community, and I'm committed to leading with honesty. If I seem stressed, I want you to know it's not your fault, and it's not a sign that I don't trust you. It means I need to lean on your wisdom and support—just as you lean on mine. We are in this together."

A teacher from the math department raised her hand. "I appreciate you saying this," she said. "I've felt stressed, too. It helps to know we're not alone." Another staff member nodded vigorously. The reading coach, who rarely spoke up in large groups, cleared his throat and said, "It makes a difference to hear you acknowledge it. Maybe we can set up a staff committee to help prioritize new initiatives, so none of us—yourself included—feels so overwhelmed."

Rita smiled, relief mingling with gratitude. Others chimed in—ideas about rotating responsibilities for certain events, sharing resources online to reduce last-minute scrambles, and even carving out a monthly "Wellness Afternoon" when students had an assembly, so teachers and leaders could catch their breath and plan collaboratively. The conversation was honest and real. No one expected Rita to be perfect; they wanted her to be authentic and approachable.

In the weeks that followed, small changes took hold. Rita updated the weekly staff bulletin with not only school news but also a quick note about how she was managing her workload, and she encouraged teachers to do the same. They began exchanging tips: how to streamline lesson planning, how to request assistance earlier rather than burning out alone, how to shift non-urgent tasks to a calmer time. Transparency bred empathy, and empathy fostered a sense of shared mission.

Gradually, Rita noticed a shift in atmosphere. Teachers weren't just following directives; they were working alongside her, bringing forth solutions she might never have seen from her isolated vantage point. Parents sensed the camaraderie and collaboration and felt reassured. Students, seeing calmer adults, seemed more at ease themselves. The entire ecosystem of Lakeside Middle School benefited from Rita's willingness to lead authentically through her own struggles.

In this way, the lessons from Chapter Eight took shape. By risking vulnerability, Rita did not lose respect—she gained it. By sharing her insufficiencies, she did not undermine her leadership—she strengthened it. Through honesty and transparency, Rita and her team built trust, understanding, and a more resilient community, proving that honest leadership, even in moments of difficulty, can illuminate a path forward for everyone.

CHAPTER NINE

Adapt or Falter: When Your Leadership Style Needs to Change

The world we live in is constantly evolving, and nowhere is this more evident than in leadership. Every day, new challenges, insights, and expectations arise, challenging us to adapt or risk becoming ineffective. As leaders, the ability to adapt isn't just a nice-to-have; it's essential. While consistency and reliability are important qualities in a leader, so too is the flexibility to adjust your approach in response to the unique needs of each situation. Sticking rigidly to one style, especially when circumstances shift, can hinder your growth and impact your effectiveness.

Adapting your leadership style doesn't mean abandoning your values or pretending to be someone you're not. Rather, it's about expanding your range, finding new ways to connect with your team, and being responsive to changing demands. In this chapter, we'll explore why adaptability is crucial in leadership, how to recognize when a change in style is needed, and practical strategies to help you adjust your approach without losing your authenticity.

Why Adaptability is Essential in Leadership

Adaptability is the hallmark of resilient, forward-thinking leaders. Leaders who embrace flexibility can adjust their approach to fit various situations, personalities, and challenges, making them more effective, more relatable, and more impactful. Here are some key reasons why adaptability is critical in leadership:

1. **Supporting Individual and Collective Growth**

   Every team is made up of individuals with unique strengths, needs, and working styles. An adaptable leader recognizes that a "one-size-fits-all" approach limits potential. Instead, they tailor their leadership style to support each person, meeting individuals where they are while keeping the broader team moving forward.

   This might involve being more hands-on with a new team member who needs guidance, while giving greater autonomy to a seasoned employee who thrives on independence. Flexibility in leadership allows each person to contribute their best, fostering both personal and collective success.

   Adaptability also means creating an environment where growth is encouraged—both for individuals and the team as a whole. Leaders who embrace innovation and experimentation unlock potential by encouraging new ideas and supporting calculated risk-taking. When leaders show they are open to different approaches, it encourages teams to innovate without fear of failure.

Example:

I encouraged innovation within my staff through a professional learning community (PLC) initiative centered on collaborative experimentation. Teachers identified areas where they could take bold steps to improve student outcomes. Some piloted flipped classrooms, while others introduced project-based learning. We created space for reflection and celebrated both successes and lessons learned from setbacks. This culture of shared learning not only improved student engagement but also reignited the team's passion for teaching.

Key Practices:

- Adjust your leadership style based on individual strengths and needs.
- Empower team members to experiment, innovate, and learn from both successes and failures.
- Celebrate personal growth and team progress—big or small.

2. **Navigating Change with Confidence**

Change is an unavoidable aspect of leadership—whether it's shifting organizational goals, adopting new technologies, or responding to evolving community needs. Leaders who resist change risk falling behind, while those who embrace it set their teams up for long-term success.

Adaptable leaders view change not as a disruption but as an opportunity to refine processes, solve problems creatively, and strengthen their team. They stay focused on the organization's vision, while adjusting plans as needed. This flexibility prevents stagnation and fosters a team culture that is agile, solutions-oriented, and forward-thinking.

Example:

During a district-wide curriculum shift, I led my team through the transition by keeping communication open, listening to concerns, and making adjustments based on their feedback. Rather than forcing immediate compliance, we phased in the changes gradually. We empowered teachers to test new strategies, shared success stories across the team, and provided extra support to those who needed it. This approach helped the team embrace the transition rather than resist it.

Key Practices:

- Stay informed about organizational and industry changes.
- Communicate openly about transitions, involving your team in the process.
- Remain flexible, adjusting plans as new information emerges.

3. **Cultivating Resilience and Stability**

Leadership is not only about guiding a team when things are going well—it's also about steadying the ship when challenges arise. Adaptable leaders build resilience by staying calm and solution-focused when faced with uncertainty or setbacks. Their composure provides reassurance to the team, creating a culture of stability and trust.

> Leadership is not only about guiding a team when things are going well—it's also about steadying the ship when challenges arise.

Resilient leaders don't avoid problems—they confront them head-on, adjusting their approach when obstacles demand it. They encourage their teams to do the same, viewing difficulties as part of the growth journey rather than as failures.

Example:

When a sudden budget cut forced our school to reduce programs, I worked closely with staff to prioritize key initiatives and creatively reallocate resources. Rather than allowing panic to set in, we focused on what we could control. I made it a point to keep the team informed, involve them in problem-solving, and highlight the progress we were still making. This resilience helped maintain morale and reinforced our collective commitment to serving students.

Key Practices:

- Model composure during uncertainty—your team will follow your lead.
- Encourage a problem-solving mindset, focusing on what can be done rather than what's been lost.
- Reinforce long-term goals while adapting short-term plans as needed.

Adaptability is more than simply reacting to change—it's the foundation of effective leadership. Leaders who support individual and team growth, navigate change with confidence, and model resilience create environments in which people thrive. When teams see that the leader is both flexible and steady, they gain the courage to innovate, grow, and face challenges together.

Recognizing When It's Time to Change Your Leadership Style

Knowing when to adjust your leadership style is as important as knowing how to do it. There are specific signs and scenarios that can signal the need for a change. Here are a few indicators that it may be time to reassess your approach:

1. **Declining Team Morale or Engagement**

    If you notice that team morale is dropping, or if engagement has waned, it could be a sign that your current leadership style isn't resonating with the team. Take note of body language in meetings, participation levels, and general energy. A disengaged team may need a different approach to reinvigorate their sense of purpose and motivation.

2. **Feedback Indicating Misalignment**

Direct feedback from your team, peers, or supervisors can offer valuable insights into areas where you may need to adjust. If you're hearing that your approach feels overly controlling, too hands-off, or misaligned with the team's needs, it's worth considering a change. Embrace feedback as an opportunity to grow and adapt.

3. **New Challenges or Shifts in Objectives**

Sometimes, changes in project goals, organizational strategy, or external factors necessitate a shift in leadership. A team working under a tight deadline might need a more directive style, while a group in the early stages of a creative project might benefit from a more collaborative, hands-off approach.

4. **Personal Feelings of Ineffectiveness or Frustration**

If you're feeling frustrated or ineffective, it may be that your current leadership style is not suited to the task or team dynamic. Instead of pushing harder, take a step back and assess whether a shift in approach might yield better results. Feelings of stagnation or dissatisfaction are often signs that an adjustment could be beneficial.

5. **Team Growth and Development**

As your team grows and develops, their needs change as well. A team that once needed close guidance may now be capable of working more independently. Recognizing these shifts and allowing team members more autonomy can foster continued growth and engagement.

Strategies for Adapting Your Leadership Style

Adaptability requires a mindset of flexibility, openness, and curiosity. Here are practical strategies for adapting your leadership style while staying true to your core values:

1. **Embrace Situational Leadership**

    Situational leadership is a model that suggests leaders should adjust their approach based on the readiness and competence of their team members. This style involves assessing the needs of the situation and adapting accordingly. For example, when working with a new team, you may need to provide more structure and guidance. With a more experienced team, a delegative style might be more effective. How to apply it:

    1. Start by evaluating the task at hand and the team member's familiarity or expertise in handling similar tasks.
    2. Consider whether the individual needs guidance, encouragement, or simply the freedom to execute.
    3. Adjust your level of involvement based on their confidence and capabilities. Be hands-on when they need support and hands-off when they need autonomy.

    By practicing situational leadership, you become adept at reading situations and choosing the style that best fits, ultimately enhancing your impact.

2. **Seek Continuous Feedback**

    Feedback is a powerful tool for self-awareness and growth. Regularly seeking input from your team and peers allows you to gauge how well your leadership style is meeting their needs. Create open channels for feedback, whether through anonymous surveys, one-on-one check-ins, or team discussions, and use their insights to inform your approach. How to apply it:

1. Set up regular feedback sessions that are both informal (like quick check-ins) and formal (structured reviews).
2. Ask specific questions, such as, *"Is there something I could be doing differently to better support you?"* or *"How can I help you reach your goals?"*
3. Listen carefully without interrupting or getting defensive, and thank team members for their honesty.
4. After receiving feedback, take time to reflect on it and consider concrete changes to your approach.

3. Develop Emotional Intelligence

Emotional intelligence (EQ) is the ability to understand and manage your own emotions, as well as the emotions of others. A high EQ helps you adapt because it enables you to respond empathetically, stay calm under pressure, and adjust your tone and style based on the situation. Practice active listening, empathy, and self-reflection to enhance your EQ, which will naturally make you a more adaptable leader. How to apply it:

1. Practice active listening by focusing fully on the speaker, acknowledging their emotions, and responding thoughtfully.
2. Develop self-awareness by noting your emotional triggers and how they affect your decisions and interactions.
3. Practice empathy by putting yourself in others' shoes, which helps you tailor your approach based on their perspectives and feelings.
4. Use self-regulation techniques like deep breathing or mental reframing to stay composed in challenging situations.

4. Stay Curious and Open to Learning

Adaptability requires a willingness to learn and try new things. Leaders who are open to learning, unafraid of experimentation, and curious about new ideas are naturally more flexible. Approach each day with a learner's mindset, viewing every experience as a chance to expand your skills and understanding. Be open to exploring new management techniques, embracing diverse perspectives, and accepting that there is always room for growth. How to apply it:

1. Dedicate time each week to reading leadership articles, attending workshops, or exploring case studies that present alternative approaches.
2. Ask your team for new ideas and actively consider how you could implement them, even if they differ from your usual methods.
3. Embrace mistakes as learning opportunities rather than setbacks. Reflect on what went wrong, what you learned, and how you can improve next time.
4. Seek out mentors or colleagues who can provide fresh perspectives on how you can approach challenges differently.

5. Recognize and Manage Your Ego

Sometimes, our own egos can prevent us from adapting. We may hold on to a certain way of leading because it's comfortable or aligns with our self-image. Recognize when your ego may be getting in the way and consciously set it aside. Remind yourself that adaptability doesn't compromise your leadership; it strengthens it. True

> Recognize when your ego may be getting in the way and consciously set it aside.

leadership isn't about rigidly defending a particular style; it's about being responsive to the needs of those you lead. How to apply it:

1. Before making decisions, ask yourself if your ego is influencing your choice. Are you prioritizing your way because it's best for the team or because it feels most comfortable?
2. Be open to admitting when you don't have all the answers. Encourage input and acknowledge the expertise of your team.
3. Remind yourself that shifting your style isn't a sign of weakness but of strength and adaptability. It shows that you prioritize results and team well-being over personal pride.

6. Use Reflection as a Tool for Adaptation

Take time to reflect on your experiences, challenges, and successes regularly. Reflective practice allows you to learn from your interactions, identify patterns, and understand what works and what doesn't. By making reflection a regular part of your routine, you'll be better equipped to assess when a change in style is needed and more open to making adjustments. How to apply it:

1. Schedule a weekly or monthly reflection period during which you review recent experiences, challenges, and successes.
2. Use a journal to jot insights, questions, or patterns you've observed in your leadership.
3. Consider asking yourself reflective questions, such as, "What could I have done differently to improve the outcome?" or "Was my leadership style effective in that situation?"
4. Make small, targeted adjustments based on your reflections, and evaluate their effectiveness over time.

7. **Experiment with Different Approaches**

Sometimes, the best way to grow is to step out of your comfort zone and try new approaches. Experiment with different leadership styles in low-stakes situations, and observe how your team responds. For example, if you're typically hands-on, try taking a step back and giving teams more independence. Use these experiments as learning opportunities, refining your approach as you go. How to apply it:

1. Identify low-risk opportunities where you can test a different approach, such as handling a routine project more collaboratively.
2. Set a specific goal for your experiment, such as enhancing team ownership or encouraging more creative problem-solving.
3. Observe and take note of your team's responses, engagement levels, and outcomes.

Afterward, debrief with your team or reflect independently to evaluate the results. Consider incorporating effective strategies into your regular approach.

A Story of Adaptation in Leadership

Consider the story of Dr. Taylor, a seasoned superintendent in a growing school district. Known for her meticulous planning, data-driven decisions, and focus on operational efficiency, Dr. Taylor had long been respected as a capable and results-oriented leader. Under her leadership, the district maintained strong academic performance and financial stability.

However, as the educational landscape began to shift—emphasizing student-centered learning, creativity, and social-emotional development—Dr. Taylor noticed cracks beginning to form. Teachers and principals, particularly younger educators passionate about innovation, began expressing frustration. They felt constrained by rigid systems and top-down directives. They craved more autonomy to pilot new instructional strategies and to respond to the diverse needs of their students.

At first, Dr. Taylor resisted. She had built her career on structure and accountability—principles that had served the district well. But declining morale, increased teacher turnover, and feedback from site leaders made it clear: what had worked in the past was no longer enough to move the district forward.

Determined to grow as a leader, Dr. Taylor took a step back and began listening more intentionally. She hosted open forums with staff, visited classrooms not to evaluate but to understand, and asked a critical question: *How can the district office better support innovation at the school level?*

What she heard was transformative. Teachers wanted freedom to experiment, principals needed flexibility to adapt policies to their communities, and everyone longed for a culture that valued creativity as much as compliance. Taking this to heart, Dr. Taylor gradually shifted her approach. She empowered school leaders to pilot new teaching models, reduced bureaucratic hurdles, and celebrated both successes and lessons learned from experimentation.

The impact was profound. Schools became more energized, teachers felt trusted, and student engagement soared. By adapting her leadership style—moving from control to collaboration—Dr. Taylor not only revitalized the district but also fostered a culture where innovation and excellence could thrive. Through her journey, she discovered that true leadership is not about holding on to what has always worked; it's about evolving to meet the ever-changing needs of those you serve.

Conclusion: The Power of Adaptability in Leadership

Adaptability is more than just a skill; it's a mindset that allows leaders to stay relevant, resilient, and responsive in a constantly changing world. As Dr. Taylor's story illustrates, the willingness to adapt doesn't just benefit the leader—it strengthens the entire team, creating an environment where people feel valued, supported, and empowered to grow.

True leadership is not about rigid adherence to a single approach. It's about having the courage to let go of what's comfortable and the wisdom to recognize when a shift is needed. Adapting your leadership style is an act of service to those you lead, an acknowledgment that their needs matter, and a commitment to meeting those needs with empathy and flexibility.

Adaptability is closely tied to self-awareness. Leaders who are in tune with their strengths, limitations, and the evolving needs of their team naturally foster a culture of continuous improvement. As leaders, we often pride ourselves on saying yes—yes to new initiatives, yes to supporting others, yes to going the extra mile. But beneath the surface of our relentless agreement lies a quiet, unspoken cost: the erosion of our time, energy, and focus. Chapter Ten delves into the transformative power of learning to say no. This chapter uncovers the critical importance of establishing healthy boundaries, not only to protect ourselves from burnout but also to model balance and prioritize what truly matters. Through stories of hard-fought lessons and practical strategies, this chapter invites leaders to confront the fear of disappointing others, redefine what it means to be a servant leader, and embrace the strength it takes to say no for the greater good. By setting boundaries, we reclaim our capacity to lead with clarity, purpose, and integrity.

Self-Reflection Prompt

Think about a recent situation where you felt your usual leadership style wasn't as effective as you hoped. Reflect on what happened, how you responded, and whether adapting your approach might have changed the outcome.

Reflection Question

What signals or feedback might you have missed that indicated a different leadership style was needed? If you were to encounter a similar situation again, what specific adjustments could you make to better support your team and meet their needs? Take a moment to jot down your thoughts and consider one or two specific ways you can practice greater adaptability in your leadership approach. These insights can help you build a more responsive and resilient leadership style.

LESSONS LEARNED

When Dr. Ramirez took the helm as superintendent of the Crescent Valley School District, she brought with her a well-earned reputation for decisive leadership and a track record of raising academic standards. In her previous district, a clear top-down approach worked brilliantly: she set ambitious goals, held everyone accountable with firm deadlines, and rewarded those who delivered results. Test scores soared, and the community applauded her no-nonsense style.

But Crescent Valley was different. Though the district had excellent teachers and supportive families, a deep-rooted culture of collaboration and shared decision-making preceded her. Dr. Ramirez's first attempts to replicate her old methods—issuing detailed directives and expecting immediate compliance—were met with hesitation. Principals grew quiet when she entered a room; teachers exchanged uncertain glances and gave polite but guarded feedback. The parent advisory council, once vocal and engaged, responded to her carefully crafted improvement plans with lukewarm interest.

At first, Dr. Ramirez assumed the issue was time. She pressed on, sending more memos and implementing tighter schedules. But as weeks passed, the distance between her office and the day-to-day life of the schools felt cavernous. The signals were subtle, but unmistakable: fewer staff members volunteered for district committees, parents asked fewer questions at town halls, and longtime principals who once led dynamic teams seemed to be going through the motions.

On a rainy Wednesday afternoon, Dr. Ramirez visited Oakwood Elementary, known for its strong teacher community. She hoped to celebrate the school's pilot literacy initiative, which had shown promising data. But in the library, as she thanked the team, the applause felt half-hearted. Instead of the eager conversation she expected, the teachers—usually brimming with ideas—simply nodded. Afterward, Ms. Bennett, an instructional coach who'd been with the district for fifteen years, approached her quietly.

"Dr. Ramirez," Ms. Bennett said softly, "I know you want us to meet these goals, and we do, too. But we're used to working problems out together. Right now, it feels like we're being told what to do, rather than invited to shape how we do it."

That gentle comment stayed with Dr. Ramirez. She realized she'd been ignoring the very essence of Crescent Valley's culture: a preference for inclusive decision-making and collaborative problem-solving. Her old leadership style, effective in a different setting, wasn't resonating here. If she continued down this path, the district might meet some targets, but it would lose the synergy and creativity that made it special. In other words, she could either adapt or falter.

That evening, Dr. Ramirez reflected on what adapting might look like. She decided to bring principals into early discussions about initiatives, asking for their perspectives before finalizing plans. She created an "innovation roundtable," inviting teacher leaders to present their ideas and co-create solutions. Instead of delivering mandates at board meetings, she started posing strategic questions— "What have we learned from this approach?"; "How can we incorporate teacher feedback earlier?"—and listening carefully to the answers.

Over the next few months, the changes were gradual but profound. Principals who had grown quiet began to speak up again, sharing insights that only they, close to the day-to-day operations of their schools, could see. Teachers who once hesitated now offered to pilot new strategies, confident their expertise would shape the rollout. Parents at advisory meetings thanked Dr. Ramirez for asking more questions and showing genuine interest in their views.

Data still mattered to Dr. Ramirez, but now she viewed it as part of a dialogue, not a unilateral directive. She realized that in Crescent Valley, the best ideas emerged from collective wisdom. By loosening her grip on control and inviting others into the decision-making process, she found a new equilibrium that honored both her vision for improvement and the district's collaborative spirit.

In the end, Dr. Ramirez's adaptability paid off. The district still pursued high standards, but now there was a shared sense of purpose that fueled innovation and sustained morale. She discovered that changing her leadership style didn't mean surrendering her goals; it meant achieving them through the strengths of the community she served. In this way, the lessons from Chapter Nine came to life. Recognizing that her old approach didn't fit Crescent Valley's culture, Dr. Ramirez adapted with empathy and openness. Instead of faltering, she guided the district toward a more authentic and inclusive path forward.

CHAPTER TEN

The Courage to Say No: Setting Boundaries in Leadership

Leadership often feels like a balancing act, with requests, challenges, and opportunities constantly competing for your time and energy. For many leaders, the instinct is to say "yes"—to help, to support, to prove their commitment. Saying "yes" feels like the path of least resistance, a way to keep things moving smoothly, maintain harmony within the team, and avoid disappointing others.

But as every leader eventually learns, this reflexive "yes" comes at a cost. The energy spent accommodating every request can lead to burnout, diminished effectiveness, and even resentment. And the truth is, saying "no" isn't about being difficult or unhelpful—it's about being strategic, intentional, and aligned with your values and goals.

This chapter explores the critical importance of setting boundaries in leadership. Saying "no" is not a weakness; it's a powerful act of clarity and focus that enables leaders to prioritize their long-term vision over immediate demands, maintain their well-being, and model healthy behavior for their teams. Let's dive into why saying "no" is essential, how to do it effectively, and how it ultimately strengthens leadership.

The Pressure to Say Yes: Why Leaders Struggle with Boundaries

Leaders often feel compelled to say "yes" for several reasons, many of which stem from a desire to serve and support others. While these motivations are rooted in good intentions, they can also become traps that hinder effectiveness. Here are some common reasons why leaders struggle to say "no":

1. **The Fear of Letting Others Down**

    Leaders are often driven by a deep sense of responsibility for their teams, colleagues, and organizations. This people-centered focus, while a strength, can also lead to a reluctance to say "no." Whether it's a teacher needing support, a board member asking for a favor, or a peer seeking collaboration, the fear of disappointing others can compel leaders to agree—even when it stretches their time and energy to the breaking point.

    Saying "yes" can feel like the safest way to preserve relationships and maintain trust. However, constantly overcommitting can have the opposite effect: missed deadlines, burnout, and a diminishing capacity to serve others well. True leadership is not about pleasing everyone—it's about making thoughtful choices that ensure you can deliver on your commitments with excellence.

Key Perspective Shift:

Saying "no" doesn't mean you're letting someone down; it often means you're protecting your capacity to serve others well in the long run.

Practical Strategies:

- Be honest when your plate is full—people respect transparency.
- Offer alternatives: "I can't take that on right now, but perhaps [someone else] could help."
- Remind yourself: *Boundaries are not barriers; they create space for your best work.*

> *Boundaries are not barriers; they create space for your best work.*

2. The Pressure to Prove Yourself

Many leaders struggle with "Superhero Syndrome"—the belief that they must handle everything alone to demonstrate their competence and value. This mindset is often fueled by imposter syndrome or the fear of being perceived as weak. Saying "yes" becomes a way to maintain control and showcase capability.

While this self-reliant approach can yield short-term results, it often leads to exhaustion, micromanagement, and diminishing trust within the team. When leaders attempt to do everything themselves, they unintentionally rob their teams of growth opportunities and undermine collective success.

Key Perspective Shift:

Asking for help or delegating is not a sign of weakness—it's a mark of confident leadership. Empowering others often leads to better outcomes than trying to carry the entire load alone.

Practical Strategies:

- Pause before saying "yes"—ask: *Is this truly my responsibility, or can someone else step up?*

- Delegate tasks as opportunities for others to develop new skills.
- Embrace the mindset that leadership is about multiplication, not martyrdom—building capacity in others is one of your greatest strengths.

3. Mistaking Busyness for Impact

In leadership, there's a subtle but dangerous trap: equating activity with productivity. The temptation to say "yes" to every meeting, initiative, or request can create the illusion of effectiveness. A packed calendar may seem like a badge of honor, but in reality, it often dilutes your focus and leaves you spread too thin to excel in areas that truly matter. This drive to "do it all" is often rooted in the desire to maintain harmony—avoiding conflict by agreeing to everything—or in the belief that busyness signals value. However, effective leadership is not about *doing the most; it's about doing what matters most.*

> **Effective leadership is not about *doing the most; it's about doing what matters most.***

Key Perspective Shift:

Saying "no" is not a rejection of others—it's a strategic choice to protect your time and energy for what drives the greatest impact.

Practical Strategies:

- Regularly evaluate your commitments—ask: *Is this contributing to my core mission, or is it a distraction?*
- Prioritize deep work—dedicating time to the few responsibilities that create lasting change.

- Normalize the idea within your team that sometimes saying "no" is the healthiest "yes"—to your well-being and your highest priorities.

True leadership is not measured by how much you say "yes" to, but by your ability to discern what deserves your best attention. Saying "no" is not an act of rejection—it's an act of stewardship, protecting your capacity to lead with excellence and intention. The most effective leaders are those who have the courage to set boundaries, empower others, and focus their time where it matters most.

Why Saying No Is a Leadership Superpower

Contrary to common misconceptions, saying "no" is not about being inflexible or uncooperative—it's about protecting your time, energy, and priorities so you can focus on what truly matters. Here's why saying "no" is an essential leadership skill:

1. **Protecting Your Vision and Priorities**

    Effective leadership requires clarity and focus. Every "yes" you give pulls time and energy from the work that drives real impact. Saying "no" is not about shutting doors—it's about keeping the right doors open. It safeguards your ability to prioritize the initiatives, goals, and values that truly align with your long-term vision.

    Without boundaries, leaders can easily become reactive—chasing every request, initiative, or meeting—at the cost of their strategic direction. Over time, this "yes to everything" mindset can dilute your efforts and prevent you from making meaningful progress on the things that matter most.

Key Shift:

Saying "no" is not rejection—it's redirection. It keeps your focus on what moves the needle for your organization.

Practical Application:

- Regularly revisit your core goals—use them as a filter for decisions.
- Before committing, ask: *Does this align with our vision? Will it advance our key priorities?*
- Communicate your "no" with clarity and respect: *"This is a great idea, but it doesn't align with our current focus. Let's revisit it later."*

2. Sustaining Your Energy and Well-Being

Leadership is a long game, and burnout is a very real threat. The pressure to meet expectations, support your team, and pursue every opportunity can lead to exhaustion—diminishing both your effectiveness and your passion. Saying "no" is an act of self-leadership. It's a recognition that you cannot serve others well if you are depleted.

Saying "no" allows you to preserve your mental, emotional, and physical capacity so you can lead with clarity and energy. Leaders who prioritize their well-being model sustainable leadership, showing their teams that success doesn't require sacrificing health.

Key Shift:

Self-care is not selfish—it's strategic. A rested, healthy leader is a better leader.

> Self-care is not selfish—it's strategic. A rested, healthy leader is a better leader.

Practical Application:

- Protect time on your calendar for rest, reflection, and family—schedule it like any other priority.
- Practice small "no" moments: decline non-essential meetings, reduce email responsiveness after hours, or delegate lower-priority tasks.
- View "no" as protecting your capacity to give your best yes to what truly matters.

3. **Building Credibility and Modeling Boundaries**

Leaders who say "yes" to everything can appear scattered or uncertain—lacking the clarity and conviction that inspire trust. In contrast, leaders who say "no" with intention demonstrate strength and decisiveness. They signal that they are clear on their goals, confident in their judgment, and willing to make difficult choices. Moreover, when leaders model healthy boundaries, it gives teams permission to do the same. It fosters a culture in which people feel empowered to prioritize their workload, protect their well-being, and focus on meaningful work—without guilt.

Key Shift:

Saying "no" is not a weakness—it's a signal of focused, value-driven leadership.

Practical Application:

- Be transparent when declining requests—explain the "why" behind your decision to build trust.
- Encourage your team to prioritize their work and set boundaries; celebrate when they push back thoughtfully.

- Reinforce that saying "no" is not failure—it's leadership in action.

Saying "no" is not about closing doors—it's about leading with clarity, protecting your energy, and empowering your team. The most effective leaders are those who know that every thoughtful "no" creates space for their best "yes."

How to Know When to Say No

The decision to say "no" isn't always straightforward, especially in high-pressure environments. However, by considering the following factors, you can develop a framework for making thoughtful decisions:

1. **Align with Your Core Values**

    Ask yourself: *Does this request align with my values and goals?* If the answer is no, then saying "yes" may take you further from what matters most. Your values are your compass, guiding you toward meaningful work and relationships.

2. **Consider the Opportunity Cost**

    Every "yes" is a "no" to something else. When evaluating a request, consider what you'll have to sacrifice if you say "yes." Will it pull you away from a critical project, personal time, or an opportunity to rest and recharge?

3. **Assess Your Capacity**

    Be honest about your current bandwidth. Even if a request aligns with your goals, saying "yes" may not be feasible if you're already stretched too thin. Overcommitting diminishes your ability to deliver quality results.

4. **Evaluate the Impact**

Will saying "yes" have a meaningful impact, or is it a low-priority task that could be delegated? Focus on the actions that drive the most value for your team and organization.

The Art of Saying No with Clarity and Empathy

Saying "no" doesn't have to be harsh or dismissive. When done with clarity and empathy, it can preserve relationships and maintain trust. Here's how to say "no" effectively:

1. **Be Direct and Honest**

When saying "no," avoid vague language or excessive justifications. Be clear about your decision and the reason behind it. For example:

Instead of: *"I'll try to fit this in, but I'm not sure I can."*

Say: *"I appreciate you asking, but I can't commit to this right now due to other priorities."*

2. **Express Appreciation**

Acknowledge the person's request and the trust they've placed in you. Showing appreciation softens the impact of a "no" and reinforces mutual respect. For example:

"Thank you for thinking of me for this project. I'm honored that you value my input."

3. **Offer an Alternative**

If possible, suggest another solution or delegate the request. This demonstrates your willingness to help while staying aligned with your priorities. For example:

"I'm unable to take this on, but I believe [Colleague's Name] would be a great fit."

4. Maintain Empathy

Saying "no" can be difficult for both parties. Show empathy by acknowledging the other person's needs and concerns, even if you can't fulfill the request. For example:

"I understand how important this is, and I wish I could help directly. Let's brainstorm other ways to get this done."

Avoiding the People-Pleaser Trap

People-pleasing can be a major obstacle to setting boundaries, especially for leaders who value harmony and relationships. Here's how to overcome the urge to please everyone:

1. Reframe "No" as a Positive

Saying "no" isn't a rejection of the person—it's a commitment to what's most important. Remind yourself that every "no" allows you to say "yes" to something more meaningful.

2. Focus on the Bigger Picture

Consider how your decision impacts the team or organization as a whole. By prioritizing long-term goals over short-term demands, you're ultimately serving the greater good.

3. Practice Saying No in Low-Stakes Situations

Build confidence by practicing "no" in smaller, less critical scenarios. Over time, you'll develop the skills and self-assurance to set boundaries in higher-pressure situations.

Delegating Without Guilt

Delegation is a powerful way to say "no" while ensuring that important work still gets done. Here's how to delegate effectively:

1. **Choose the Right Person**
Match the task with someone who has the skills and capacity to handle it. Delegating to the right person increases the likelihood of success and builds trust within the team.

2. **Provide Clear Instructions**
Set team members up for success by providing clear expectations, resources, and timelines. For example:
"I'd like you to take the lead on this project. Here's what success looks like, and let's check in next week to discuss progress."

3. **Empower Your Team**
Delegation isn't just about offloading tasks—it's an opportunity to develop the team's skills and confidence. Encourage autonomy and celebrate their successes.

4. **Let Go of Perfectionism**
Resist the urge to micromanage or expect the task to be done exactly as you would. Trust your team's abilities and focus on the results, not the process.

Conclusion: The Power of Boundaries in Leadership

Saying "no" isn't just about protecting your time—it's about honoring your values, focusing on what matters, and leading with intention. Boundaries are not barriers; they're bridges to sustainable leadership and meaningful impact. By learning to say "no" with clarity and empathy, you create space for the "yeses" that align with your vision and goals. As you continue your leadership journey, remember that the courage to say "no" is a gift to yourself, and the people you serve. It allows you to lead with focus, energy, and authenticity.

Reflection Prompt

Think about a time when you said "yes" to something you wished you had declined. What motivated your decision, and how did it impact your priorities? Looking ahead, what boundaries can you set to ensure your "yeses" align with your values and long-term goals?

LESSONS LEARNED

Hannah had been principal of Forestview Elementary for almost two years. When she first took the job, she saw herself as the ultimate problem-solver—someone who would never let a question go unanswered or a concern remain unresolved. If a teacher needed help modifying a lesson plan, Hannah would rewrite it herself. If a parent asked for a special meeting after hours, Hannah would stay late. If the district office called for a new committee member, Hannah volunteered before anyone else could blink.

At first, she felt proud of her willingness to say "yes" to everyone. Her reputation soared: staff, parents, and even the district office knew they could count on Principal Hannah for everything. But over time, she noticed a heavy fatigue settling in. She spent so many evenings at school events that she rarely saw her own family at dinner. Emails piled up in her inbox until midnight, and she caught herself snapping at small things—like a teacher needing a second explanation—because she was stretched so thin. Hannah felt frazzled, constantly behind, and worried that she'd burn out before she ever truly hit her stride as a leader.

One rainy Monday afternoon, Hannah realized she'd agreed to three overlapping commitments: leading a parent workshop on literacy strategies, reviewing a complex budget proposal, and chairing the district's new technology implementation committee. Each of these tasks mattered, but did all of them need her personal involvement?

Sitting alone in her office as the hallway lights dimmed, Hannah remembered the lessons from this chapter about setting boundaries. She had to face a hard truth: sometimes, effective leadership meant saying "no." Not because she didn't care, but because agreeing to everything made her less effective overall. By stretching herself too thin, she risked making rushed decisions and offering half-hearted support.

The next morning, Hannah took a small but courageous step. When the district office emailed once again, asking her to join yet another task force—this time on extended-day programming—she paused before responding. Previously, she would have typed "Yes, count me in!" without a second thought. Now, she reflected: *Will this use of my time help me better serve my school's core priorities? What will I have to give up to do this well?* The answer was clear. She would have to sacrifice hours that should go to teacher coaching and supporting her school's reading initiative. So Hannah typed a respectful but firm response: "I appreciate the invitation, but I must decline so I can stay focused on our school's immediate goals. Thank you for understanding."

With a click of "send," she felt a strange mix of relief and uncertainty. Would the district think less of her? Would she lose respect? To her surprise, the reply was gracious: "Understood—thanks for letting us know." Nothing collapsed. In fact, by protecting her time, Hannah freed herself to give better support where it mattered most.

Emboldened by this experience, Hannah began to set boundaries elsewhere. She told the after-school clubs coordinator she couldn't attend every meeting in person, but she'd be happy to review their proposals monthly instead. When a parent requested three separate after-hours conferences in one week, Hannah gently said she could only schedule one and encouraged the parent to email or speak with the classroom teacher for additional updates. At staff meetings, if a new initiative felt like it didn't align with their strategic goals, Hannah no longer automatically said "yes." Instead, she asked, *"Is this the best use of our team's time right now?"* If it wasn't, she calmly declined or postponed the request.

Over time, something remarkable happened. Hannah's staff began to respect her boundaries. Teachers became more thoughtful about when to escalate issues to the principal; they solved more problems among themselves first. Parents understood that while Hannah valued their concerns, she had to balance many priorities. Rather than losing respect, Hannah gained it. People saw that she made clearer decisions and followed through on her existing commitments with more care and consistency. Her presence felt calmer, her attention more focused, and the quality of her support richer.

By learning to say "no" strategically and kindly, Hannah created space for what truly mattered—supporting her teachers' instruction, following up on student interventions, and developing meaningful relationships with families. She learned that her "no" was not a rejection of the school community's needs but a way to ensure she could meet them more effectively in the long run.

In this way, the lessons from Chapter Ten came to life. Setting boundaries did not weaken Hannah's leadership; it strengthened it. By courageously declining tasks that detracted from her core mission, she preserved her energy, clarified her priorities, and ultimately became a more confident, respected leader.

CHAPTER ELEVEN

The Role of Emotional Agility: Navigating Complexity with Grace

Leadership is never a straight line. It's a labyrinth of decisions, relationships, challenges, and triumphs, each one colored by a kaleidoscope of emotions. The ability to navigate this emotional complexity isn't just a bonus for leaders; it's a necessity. This chapter delves into the concept of emotional agility—a skill that goes beyond emotional intelligence, teaching leaders how to sit with discomfort, face ambivalence, and find clarity amidst chaos.

While emotional intelligence focuses on recognizing, understanding, and managing emotions, emotional agility takes it a step further. It's about engaging with emotions—both yours and others'—in a way that's constructive and adaptive. It's the ability to move through conflicting feelings with grace, respond thoughtfully rather than react impulsively, and find resilience in the face of setbacks. Emotional agility isn't about bypassing tough emotions or forcing optimism; it's about using those emotions as a compass, guiding you toward growth, insight, and effective action.

This chapter offers strategies to help you embrace emotional agility as a cornerstone of your leadership, equipping you to lead with clarity and grace, even in the most uncertain times.

Emotional Agility vs. Emotional Intelligence

To understand emotional agility, it's important to differentiate it from emotional intelligence (EI). While the two concepts overlap, they serve distinct purposes in leadership.

Emotional intelligence is the ability to recognize and manage emotions—both your own and others'. It involves self-awareness, self-regulation, empathy, and social skills. Leaders with high emotional intelligence can navigate interpersonal dynamics effectively, build strong relationships, and maintain composure under pressure.

Emotional agility, on the other hand, is the ability to navigate the full spectrum of emotions—especially conflicting or uncomfortable ones—with mindfulness and intention. It's not just about identifying emotions but also about engaging with them productively. Emotional agility involves:

- Accepting emotions without judgment (even the messy, unpleasant ones).
- Pausing to understand what emotions are telling you rather than reacting impulsively.
- Making intentional choices about how to respond based on your values and goals.

Think of emotional intelligence as the foundation and emotional agility as the advanced practice. While EI helps you understand emotions, agility teaches you how to move through them constructively.

THE ROLE OF EMOTIONAL AGILITY

The Power of Sitting with Discomfort

> Emotional agility begins with the willingness to sit with that discomfort rather than avoid or suppress it.

Leaders often feel pressure to have answers, exude confidence, and project control. But leadership is full of discomfort—uncertainty about decisions, frustration with setbacks, and the weight of responsibility. Emotional agility begins with the willingness to sit with that discomfort rather than avoid or suppress it.

Why Avoidance Backfires: The Hidden Costs of Suppressing Emotions

Avoiding uncomfortable emotions—whether it's fear, frustration, disappointment, or self-doubt—may feel like the easier path in the moment. Leaders often push emotions aside to maintain composure, keep the team moving forward, or simply because they believe emotions have no place in leadership. However, this avoidance is rarely a long-term solution. In fact, it often backfires, creating deeper challenges down the line.

1. **Suppressed Emotions Don't Disappear – They Escalate**
   Emotions that are ignored or buried don't simply vanish; they linger beneath the surface, often growing stronger over time. What begins as mild frustration can snowball into resentment. Anxiety can morph into chronic stress. Left unchecked, these emotions can erode mental health, leading to burnout, exhaustion, or emotional detachment from your work.

2. **Emotional Leakage: When Avoidance Shows Up Anyway**

Even when leaders believe they are keeping their emotions hidden, those feelings often surface in unintended ways. Suppressed anger can come out as passive-aggressiveness. Unaddressed anxiety might lead to micromanaging. Fear of failure can result in indecision or overreacting to small mistakes. These "leaks" can confuse teams and erode trust—especially when your outward behavior doesn't align with your message.

3. **Missed Insights and Growth Opportunities**

Emotions are not obstacles to leadership; they are signals. They often reveal deeper truths about your values, your boundaries, or areas where growth is needed. Avoiding emotions cuts off access to this valuable information. Leaders who lean into discomfort can use those feelings to sharpen their self-awareness, improve decision-making, and lead with empathy.

4. **Damage to Relationships and Team Culture**

When leaders avoid their own emotions, they often dismiss or downplay the emotions of others. Over time, this can create a culture in which people feel unheard, undervalued, or afraid to speak up. Emotional avoidance sends the message—whether intentional or not—that emotions are a weakness, when in reality, they are a core part of human connection and trust.

The Alternative: Facing Emotions with Courage Emotionally healthy leaders recognize that discomfort is not the enemy—avoidance is. Growth comes when you face emotions, process them, and respond thoughtfully.

- **Pause and Acknowledge:** Name the emotion—*I'm feeling anxious about this decision.*

- **Get Curious:** Ask *Why is this emotion showing up? What is it telling me?*
- **Respond, Don't React:** Once emotions are acknowledged, you can choose a thoughtful response rather than a knee-jerk reaction.

Ultimately, avoiding emotions may offer temporary relief, but facing them builds resilience, clarity, and deeper connection—with yourself and those you lead. Let's lean in a little deeper into how to face your emotions with courage.

Responding Thoughtfully vs. Reacting Impulsively

In high-stress situations, it's easy to fall into reactive patterns—snapping at a team member, making a rash decision, or retreating into avoidance. Emotional agility helps you break free from these knee-jerk responses, empowering you to respond thoughtfully and intentionally.

The Pause Principle The key to thoughtful responses is the ability to pause. In the heat of the moment, a pause creates a buffer between the stimulus (what's happening) and your response. It allows you to assess the situation, understand your emotions, and choose a course of action aligned with your values.

Steps to Practice the Pause:

1. **Acknowledge the Emotion**

    Notice and name what you're feeling: anger, frustration, anxiety, etc. Naming the emotion helps you distance yourself from it and prevents it from overwhelming your response.

2. **Take a Breath**
Engage in a simple grounding technique, such as deep breathing or counting to five. This calms your nervous system and clears your mind.

3. **Ask Yourself Key Questions**
Reflect on questions like:

- *What am I feeling, and why?*
- *What does this situation need from me right now?*
- *What response aligns with my values and goals?*

4. **Respond with Intention**
Choose your response based on the insights gained during the pause. Ensure your actions reflect the leader you want to be.

Example in Action

Imagine a team member delivers feedback that feels critical of your leadership. Your initial reaction might be defensiveness or frustration. Instead of reacting impulsively, you pause. You acknowledge, *"I'm feeling defensive because this feedback challenges how I see myself as a leader."* You take a breath, remind yourself that feedback is an opportunity for growth, and respond with curiosity: *"Thank you for sharing this. Can you help me understand what led to that perception?"* This thoughtful response fosters trust and collaboration.

Recovering from Setbacks with Resilience

Setbacks are inevitable in leadership. Whether it's a failed project, a strained relationship, or personal disappointment, emotional agility equips you to bounce back stronger and wiser.

THE ROLE OF EMOTIONAL AGILITY

Reframing Setbacks A core component of emotional agility is reframing setbacks as opportunities for growth. Instead of seeing failure as a reflection of your inadequacy, view it as a steppingstone for improvement. Ask yourself:

- *What can I learn from this experience?*
- *What strengths did I demonstrate during this challenge?*
- *How can I apply these lessons moving forward?*

Reframing doesn't minimize the difficulty of setbacks; it shifts your focus from the problem to the potential.

Practicing Self-Compassion Resilience isn't about being tough on yourself—it's about treating yourself with kindness in the face of setbacks. Self-compassion involves three elements:

1. **Mindfulness:** Acknowledge your feelings without exaggerating or suppressing them.
2. **Self-Kindness:** Speak to yourself as you would a friend, with encouragement and understanding.
3. **Common Humanity:** Remind yourself that everyone experiences challenges; you're not alone.

For example, after a tough board meeting, instead of saying, "I blew it," try, "That was hard, but I did my best, and I'll use this experience to prepare even better next time."

Practical Exercises to Develop Emotional Agility

Building emotional agility is a practice that requires intention and repetition. Here are exercises to help you strengthen this skill:

1. **The Emotional Check-In**
   Set aside time each day to reflect on your emotions. Ask yourself:

   + *What emotions am I experiencing today?*
   + *What triggered these emotions?*
   + *How am I responding to them? By regularly checking in, you become more attuned to your emotional patterns and better equipped to navigate them.*

2. **Journaling for Clarity**
   Writing about your emotions can help you process them constructively. Use prompts such as:

   + *What am I feeling right now, and why?*
   + *What does this emotion reveal about my values or concerns?*
   + *What action can I take that aligns with my goals? Journaling helps you turn emotional noise into actionable insights.*

3. **The "Values Compass" Exercise**
   When faced with a challenging decision or emotion, use your values as a guide. Write down your top three leadership values (e.g., integrity, collaboration, growth). Ask yourself:

   + *What choice reflects these values?*
   + *How can I stay true to my principles in this situation? This exercise ensures that your responses align with your deeper purpose.*

4. **Mindfulness Meditation**
   Mindfulness practices, such as prayer or meditation, improve your ability to observe emotions without becoming consumed by them. Spend 5–10 minutes each day focusing on your breath and observing

your thoughts and feelings. Over time, this practice enhances your ability to pause and respond thoughtfully.

5. Role-Playing Difficult Conversations

Practice navigating emotionally charged situations by role-playing with a trusted colleague or coach. For example:

- Choose a challenging scenario (e.g., delivering constructive feedback or responding to criticism).
- Practice using the Pause Principle and responding with clarity and empathy.
- Reflect on what went well and where you can improve.

The Ripple Effect of Emotional Agility in Leadership

Leaders who cultivate emotional agility create a ripple effect throughout their teams and organizations. Here's how this skill transforms leadership and team dynamics:

1. Fostering a Culture of Resilience

When leaders model emotional agility, they inspire their teams to approach challenges with the same mindset. A resilient team doesn't shy away from discomfort; it faces setbacks with curiosity, adaptability, and a commitment to growth.

2. Enhancing Psychological Safety

Emotionally agile leaders create environments where team members feel safe expressing their emotions and ideas. This psychological safety fosters innovation, collaboration, and trust.

3. **Building Stronger Relationships**

By engaging with emotions thoughtfully, leaders deepen their connections with others. Emotional agility enhances empathy and understanding, strengthening relationships at all levels.

Emotional agility is a vital tool for navigating the complexities of leadership, but it's only one piece of the puzzle. In the next chapter, we'll explore how the questions leaders ask can shape their teams, spark innovation, and drive meaningful change. By pairing emotional agility with powerful inquiry, you'll unlock new possibilities for growth, connection, and success.

Reflection Prompt

Think about a recent situation where you felt conflicted or overwhelmed by emotions. How did you respond, and how might emotional agility have changed the outcome? What practices can you adopt to navigate similar situations with more clarity and grace in the future?

LESSONS LEARNED

When Ms. Carter became principal of Cedar Grove Elementary, she had confidence in her communication skills and prided herself on her emotional intelligence. She knew how to read a room, sense when a teacher was feeling discouraged, and offer a supportive comment to lift the mood. But in her third year as principal, Ms. Carter confronted a complexity she hadn't yet faced.

A proposed boundary change by the district threatened to reshuffle attendance zones, potentially moving a portion of Cedar Grove's students to another school. The district office had handed down the directive with little warning. Families were anxious. Teachers worried about losing valued colleagues if their enrollment dropped. And Ms. Carter herself wrestled with a mix of emotions: frustration at not being consulted more thoroughly, sadness over potentially losing familiar faces, and concern about how all of this would impact school climate and learning continuity.

An evening community forum was scheduled to discuss the boundary change. Walking into the auditorium that night, Ms. Carter felt a tightness in her chest. She recognized it as anxiety: *I need to show strength, calm, and assurance—how can I do that when I'm feeling uncertain myself?* In the past, she might have tried to mask these emotions, pushing them down and wearing a bravely neutral face. But she remembered the lessons in emotional agility— about acknowledging and working through emotions, rather than ignoring them.

Before stepping up to the microphone, she paused in a quiet corner behind the stage curtains. She named what she felt: *I'm frustrated that I don't have all the answers, I'm worried about how our community will respond, and I'm sad that some of our close-knit families might move away.* Naming these emotions calmed her a bit. Then she asked herself: *What do these feelings tell me?* They told her how deeply she cared about the students' well-being and the staff's morale. Her emotions were a sign of investment, not weakness.

Ms. Carter took three slow, mindful breaths. She remembered that emotional agility wasn't about fearing complexity but learning to move with it—like navigating a winding river rather than trying to straighten its course. She decided her approach would be honest, empathetic, and curious. She wouldn't pretend to have perfect answers, but she would strive to create a space where families and staff felt heard and supported.

As the forum began, parents stepped up to the microphone. One mother's voice shook with anger: "Why are you letting them tear our community apart?" Another parent expressed tearful worry about her child losing friendships. A teacher asked pointedly, "How can we plan our curriculum if we don't even know who our students will be?"

Each comment stirred emotions in Ms. Carter—defensiveness, sympathy, uncertainty. Instead of reacting immediately, she paused, acknowledged her emotional response internally, and then responded thoughtfully. When faced with anger, she recognized the parent's fear beneath it. "I hear how painful this feels," she said, steady and compassionate. "I'm frustrated, too. I wish we had more lead time and clearer information. Let's talk about what we can control and how we can support our children in this transition."

When someone challenged her leadership, Ms. Carter noticed a flash of defensiveness. Instead of snapping back, she took a breath and reframed it: *This teacher's criticism shows how deeply they care about stability and trust.* She responded with calm sincerity: "I understand that this uncertainty makes it hard to plan. I don't have all the answers yet, but I promise we'll gather input and share updates as soon as we learn them. Perhaps we can form a team of staff and parents to outline possible scenarios, so we feel more prepared."

By allowing herself to feel her emotions and then choosing a constructive path forward, Ms. Carter navigated the forum with grace. Although no one left the auditorium perfectly satisfied—complex changes rarely have simple resolutions—many parents thanked her for listening. A few teachers approached afterward, acknowledging how tough the evening had been and appreciating that she'd remained open, calm, and respectful.

In the following days, Ms. Carter followed through on her promise. She invited representatives from the parent community and staff to a series of planning sessions where they could anticipate possible outcomes of the boundary shift and develop strategies for maintaining relationships and continuity. This collaborative approach, fueled by empathy and thoughtful engagement, helped the community feel more resilient and united.

THE ROLE OF EMOTIONAL AGILITY

> In this way, the lessons from Chapter Eleven took shape. By practicing emotional agility—naming her feelings, finding their meaning, and responding with intention—Ms. Carter led not by suppressing complexity but by navigating it. She modeled a leadership that embraced uncertainty and emotional honesty, ultimately fostering trust, understanding, and a path forward through a challenging moment in Cedar Grove's history.

CHAPTER TWELVE

The Art of Asking the Right Questions: Unlocking Growth Through Inquiry

In the realm of leadership, one of the most underappreciated superpowers isn't the ability to provide answers—it's the ability to ask the right questions. The best leaders aren't the ones with all the solutions but those who know how to inspire their teams to uncover those solutions themselves. Thoughtful inquiry drives engagement, fosters critical thinking, and encourages innovation. It transforms leadership from directive to collaborative, empowering team members to own their ideas, decisions, and growth.

This chapter explores the transformative power of questions in leadership. From navigating conflicts to sparking creativity and uncovering hidden opportunities, the right questions can shift mindsets, deepen understanding, and unlock untapped potential. But asking the right questions isn't just about strategy; it's about fostering a culture in which curiosity is valued, assumptions are challenged, and everyone is encouraged to think expansively.

The Power of Questions in Leadership

Questions are more than just requests for information—they are tools that shape the way people think, collaborate, and problem-solve. When leaders ask thoughtful, open-ended questions, they create space for reflection, exploration, and innovation. Here's why questions are such a powerful leadership tool:

1. **Encouraging Critical Thinking**

    Questions prompt people to think deeply, analyze situations, and consider different perspectives. Instead of providing ready-made answers, leaders who ask questions encourage their teams to engage in the cognitive process of finding solutions.

2. **Empowering Teams**

    When leaders ask for input and listen to their teams' responses, they signal trust and respect. This empowers team members to take ownership of their ideas and decisions, fostering a sense of accountability and collaboration.

3. **Sparking Innovation**

    Questions challenge the status quo and encourage people to think creatively. By questioning assumptions and exploring new possibilities, leaders can unlock innovative solutions and drive progress.

4. **Building Trust and Connection**

    Asking thoughtful questions shows genuine interest in others' perspectives. This builds trust, strengthens relationships, and fosters an environment where people feel valued and heard.

The Anatomy of a Powerful Question

Not all questions are created equal. Powerful questions share certain characteristics that make them more effective at driving growth, innovation, and connection.

1. Open-Ended

Powerful questions invite expansive thinking rather than simple "yes" or "no" answers. For example:
- Instead of: *"Did you meet the deadline?"*
- Ask: *"What challenges did you face in meeting the deadline, and how can we address them?"*

2. Thought-Provoking

The best questions encourage deep reflection and push people to think beyond their immediate concerns. For example:

- *"What assumptions are we making about this problem, and are they valid?"*

3. Aligned with Goals

Effective questions are intentional, designed to guide the conversation toward meaningful insights or actions. For example:

- *"How does this decision align with our long-term vision?"*

4. Nonjudgmental

A great question fosters curiosity and exploration, not defensiveness. It should create a safe space for honest dialogue. For example:

- *"What are some alternative approaches we could consider?"*

Building a Culture of Curiosity

Curiosity is the foundation of innovation and growth. Leaders who cultivate a culture of curiosity encourage their teams to question assumptions, explore new ideas, and seek continuous improvement. Here's how to foster curiosity within your organization:

1. **Normalize Questions**

   Encourage team members to ask questions at all levels, whether in meetings, brainstorming sessions, or one-on-one conversations. Model this behavior by asking questions yourself and valuing others' input.

2. **Reward Exploration**

   Celebrate curiosity and experimentation, even when the outcomes aren't perfect. Recognize team members who challenge the status quo or propose new ideas, reinforcing that curiosity is valued.

3. **Create Safe Spaces**

   Make it clear that all questions are welcome and that there's no such thing as a "stupid question." Foster an environment where people feel comfortable sharing their thoughts without fear of judgment.

4. **Challenge Assumptions**

   Encourage your team to question assumptions regularly. For example, during planning sessions, ask:

   - "Why are we doing it this way?"
   - "What would happen if we tried a different approach?"

5. **Make Time for Reflection**

   Set aside dedicated time for your team to reflect, brainstorm, and explore ideas. Structured curiosity, like scheduled innovation sessions, can lead to breakthroughs that day-to-day operations might overlook.

Using Questions to Navigate Conflict

Conflict is an inevitable component of leadership, but the way you handle it can either exacerbate tensions or lead to resolution. Asking thoughtful questions can de-escalate conflict, uncover underlying issues, and pave the way for collaborative solutions.

1. **Clarify Perspectives**

    Conflict often arises from misunderstandings or differing perspectives. Use questions to uncover each party's point of view. For example:
    - *"Can you help me understand your concerns?"*
    - *"What's most important to you in this situation?"*

2. **Identify Root Causes**

    Surface-level conflicts often mask deeper issues. Ask probing questions to uncover the root causes. For example:

    - *"What factors are contributing to this tension?"*
    - *"How can we address the underlying challenges?"*

3. **Focus on Solutions**

    Shift the conversation from blame to collaboration by asking solution-focused questions. For example:

    - *"What would a successful outcome look like for everyone involved?"*
    - *"What steps can we take to move forward together?"*

4. **Acknowledge Emotions**

Emotions play a significant role in conflicts. Validate feelings without judgment by asking empathetic questions. For example:

- *"How are you feeling about this situation?"*
- *"What support do you need right now?"*

Unlocking Hidden Opportunities Through Inquiry

The right questions don't just solve problems—they reveal opportunities that might otherwise go unnoticed. Here's how to use inquiry to uncover hidden potential:

> **The right questions don't just solve problems—they reveal opportunities that might otherwise go unnoticed.**

1. **Explore Unmet Needs**

Ask questions that identify gaps or unmet needs within your organization or market. For example:

- *"What feedback have we received from customers that we haven't acted on yet?"*
- *"What challenges are our team members facing that haven't been addressed?"*

2. **Look for Patterns**

Encourage teams to analyze trends and patterns by asking reflective questions. For example:

- *"What themes do we see emerging from our recent projects?"*
- *"What's been consistently holding us back, and how can we overcome it?"*

3. Challenge Conventional Thinking

Push teams to think beyond traditional approaches by asking disruptive questions. For example:

- *"If we weren't limited by time or resources, how would we approach this?"*
- *"What would we do if we were starting from scratch?"*

4. Envision the Future

Guide teams to think long-term by asking visionary questions. For example:

- *"Where do we want to be in five years, and what steps can we take today to get there?"*
- *"What trends are shaping our industry, and how can we stay ahead of them?"*

Examples of Powerful Leadership Questions

To bring these concepts to life, here are examples of powerful questions you can use in various leadership scenarios:

For Problem-Solving

- *"What's the real challenge we're trying to solve here?"*
- *"What assumptions are we making, and are they valid?"*

For Team Development

- *"What skills or experiences would you like to develop, and how can I support you?"*
- *"What do you need from me to perform at your best?"*

For Innovation

- "What's a risk we haven't taken yet that might pay off?"
- "If we could wave a magic wand, what would we change about our process?"

For Reflection

- "What did we learn from this experience, and how can we apply it moving forward?"
- "What's one thing we could do differently next time?"

For Building Trust

- "What's something I might not be seeing that you think is important?"
- "How can I better support you or the team?"

Conclusion: The Transformative Power of Questions

Asking the right questions is more than a leadership strategy—it's a mindset. It's about fostering curiosity, empowering others, and unlocking potential. Questions have the power to transform not only the way you lead but also the way your team thinks, collaborates, and grows.

By embracing the art of inquiry, you create a culture where curiosity thrives, assumptions are challenged, and innovation flourishes. You become not just a problem-solver but a catalyst for growth and discovery.

The ability to ask the right questions is a cornerstone of effective leadership, but it's only part of the equation. In the next chapter, we will explore how understanding the dynamics, culture, and needs of your organization can amplify your impact. By aligning self-awareness with a broader perspective, you'll learn to lead not just individuals, but entire teams and organizations with clarity and vision.

Reflection Prompt

Think about the last major decision or challenge you faced as a leader. What questions did you ask—or not ask—that shaped the outcome? How might asking more powerful or open-ended questions have led to deeper insights or better results?

LESSONS LEARNED

Marisol, the newly appointed principal of Riverside Middle School, entered the staff meeting with a fresh mission in mind. After reading about the power of inquiry in leadership, she was determined to shift from merely providing answers to asking the kinds of questions that would unlock her team's collective wisdom.

For weeks, she'd observed the staff circling the same challenges: persistent gaps in reading comprehension among certain student groups, dwindling parent participation in school events, and a library that sat underutilized. The teachers were passionate and dedicated but seemed stuck, returning to familiar routines rather than exploring new solutions.

Instead of walking into the meeting with a detailed action plan, as she might have done in the past, Marisol decided to lead with questions. She began by acknowledging everyone's commitment and then posed a simple inquiry: "What do you think is the biggest barrier keeping some of our students from engaging deeply with reading?" She spoke calmly, paused, and waited.

At first, the staff looked surprised. Usually, Marisol would arrive with a set of recommendations to implement. Now, she was asking them to explore the root of the issue. A sixth-grade English teacher raised his hand, hesitating. "I think some students struggle because the books aren't reflecting their interests or experiences." A reading specialist nodded and added, "And maybe we don't give them enough choice in what they read."

Marisol listened, then asked a follow-up question: "How might we bring more relevance and student voice into our reading materials?" This open-ended prompt sparked a lively discussion. Teachers brainstormed ways to survey students about their interests, partner with the community library to access culturally diverse collections, or let students curate reading lists for their classmates.

Next, Marisol turned to another challenge: parent participation. Instead of chiding staff about communication strategies, she asked, "When have we seen strong parent engagement in the past, and what made those moments possible?" A counselor recalled how a family potluck night had been co-designed by parents who contributed menu ideas and activities. A math teacher mentioned the popular "Learning Night" where parents saw their children's project-based work in progress, not just at the end. Reflecting on these successes, the team realized that parents engaged more deeply when they were treated as partners and co-creators, rather than passive attendees.

Finally, Marisol addressed the underutilized library: "What would make the library a place our students and teachers naturally gravitate toward?" Ideas flowed freely: inviting local authors to speak, organizing student-led book clubs, integrating art and media production labs, and displaying student recommendations prominently. By asking "How can we..." and "What would it take to...," Marisol's questions transformed the library from a dusty corner of the building into a canvas awaiting their collective imagination.

Throughout the meeting, Marisol resisted the urge to interject her own solutions. Instead, she allowed her team's questions and responses to guide the conversation. By the end of the meeting, staff members didn't just have a list of new initiatives; they had a renewed sense of ownership and creativity. Teachers left the meeting energized, talking excitedly in the hallway about next steps.

The following month, students discovered fresh, diverse literature selections and had a say in their reading choices. Parents received invitations to co-plan events, not just attend them. The library began posting "Book Ambassadors" chosen from the student body, sparking friendly reading competitions and peer-to-peer recommendations.

All this progress stemmed from a simple yet powerful shift in Marisol's approach. Instead of arriving with predetermined fixes, she asked the right questions—open-ended, thought-provoking, and centered on the team's experiences and expertise. By doing so, she unlocked growth through inquiry, turning problems into opportunities for innovation and mutual learning.

In this way, the lessons from Chapter Twelve came to life. Marisol discovered that by leading with curiosity and inquiry, she didn't need to have all the answers. The power lay in empowering her staff to think more expansively, embrace their collective intelligence, and co-create solutions that would sustain Riverside Middle School's progress for years to come.

CHAPTER THIRTEEN

Beyond Self-Awareness: Cultivating Organizational Awareness

Leadership begins with understanding oneself, but true impact arises when that understanding expands outward—to the systems, cultures, and people that surround you. As a school leader, your world is not just a collection of individual students, teachers, and families. It's a dynamic ecosystem of relationships, values, and unwritten norms. To lead effectively, you need to go beyond *self-awareness* and cultivate a keen sense of *organizational awareness*.

Organizational awareness is more than understanding policies or departmental structures. It's about reading the unspoken rules, recognizing hidden dynamics, and aligning your leadership with the heartbeat of your school community. It's the art of seeing both the forest and the trees, navigating not just what is written in handbooks but also what is felt in hallways and classrooms. In this chapter, we'll journey into the art of organizational awareness, exploring how it transforms good leaders into great ones.

The Pulse of the School: A Principal's Journey

At the heart of organizational awareness is the ability to read the culture and dynamics of your school. To illustrate, let's walk through the journey of Melissa, a first-year principal at Evergreen Elementary School.

Melissa stepped into her role brimming with enthusiasm and a clear vision. She had spent the summer crafting strategic goals, revamping professional development plans, and refining instructional priorities. On paper, she was ready to lead Evergreen into its next chapter. But as the school year began, Melissa sensed something was off. Staff meetings felt tense, enthusiasm for her initiatives was lukewarm, and she overheard whispers of resistance in the break room. Despite her well-laid plans, Melissa's vision wasn't resonating.

One Friday afternoon, after a particularly draining staff meeting, Melissa decided to do something unconventional. She put away her to-do list and spent the day walking the hallways, chatting informally with teachers, custodians, office staff, and even a few parents picking up their kids. She asked questions—simple, open-ended ones like, "How's your day going?" or "What's something you're excited about this week?" She listened without judgment, taking mental notes of the themes that emerged.

By the end of the day, Melissa had uncovered a key piece of Evergreen's culture that her self-awareness alone hadn't revealed: trust. Or rather, a lack of it. Staff members were still reeling from the abrupt departure of the previous principal, who had implemented sweeping changes with little input. Teachers felt wary of yet another leader with big ideas, fearing their voices would again be overlooked.

Melissa realized that her first priority wasn't to implement her vision—it was to rebuild trust. She needed to meet her staff where they were, to acknowledge their hesitations, and to involve them in shaping the future. That realization marked a turning point. Melissa shifted her focus from leading for her school to leading with her school. And that made all the difference.

The Layers of Organizational Awareness

Melissa's story highlights an essential truth: understanding your school's culture and dynamics is just as important as knowing yourself. Organizational awareness operates on multiple levels, each offering valuable insights for leadership:

The Visible and the Invisible Every school has two layers of operation: the visible and the invisible. The visible includes formal structures like schedules, curricula, and policies. These are the "what" of your school—tangible elements that guide day-to-day operations.

But beneath the surface lies the invisible: the values, relationships, and emotions that truly drive behavior. This is the "how" of your school—how decisions are made, how people interact, and how trust is built or eroded. Leaders who focus solely on the visible miss the nuanced dynamics that often determine success.

For Melissa, the visible layer was her strategic plan, complete with metrics and timelines. The invisible layer, however, was the staff's lingering distrust and their need for collaboration. By tuning into this deeper layer, Melissa was able to recalibrate her approach and align her leadership with the school's true needs.

Reading the Room Organizational awareness also means developing the ability to "read the room." This involves paying attention to subtle cues—body language, tone of voice, and even the energy of a meeting. Are teachers leaning in with interest or crossing their arms in frustration? Are staff members speaking up or staying silent? These cues offer real-time feedback on your leadership and the school's morale.

During one of her listening sessions, Melissa noticed that certain staff members—those with years of experience and strong peer relationships—held significant influence among their colleagues. These informal leaders weren't on the organizational chart, but their support was critical to the success of any initiative. Recognizing their influence, Melissa began involving them in planning meetings, seeking their input and championing their ideas. This small adjustment shifted the tone of staff discussions, paving the way for greater buy-in.

Aligning Personal Growth with School Needs

As school leaders, our growth often feels personal—developing better communication, honing decision-making, or refining instructional expertise. But to be truly effective, personal growth must align with the evolving needs of your school:

Listening to the Ecosystem Your school is an ecosystem, constantly shifting in response to new challenges and opportunities. Organizational awareness requires active listening—not just to individuals, but to the collective system. This means tuning into patterns, identifying gaps, and understanding how each part of the school interacts with the whole.

Melissa found that Evergreen's culture placed a high value on professional autonomy. Teachers thrived when they felt trusted to innovate in their classrooms. Instead of imposing rigid mandates, Melissa adjusted her approach to provide flexible frameworks, allowing teachers to adapt initiatives to their unique contexts. This balance of structure and autonomy reflected her personal growth as a leader while meeting her school's cultural needs.

Balancing Vision with Reality

Leadership is often a balancing act between your vision and the reality of your school's current state. It's easy to fall into the trap of pursuing your goals at the expense of your team's capacity. Organizational awareness helps you navigate this balance, ensuring that your ambitions are both inspiring and achievable.

For Melissa, this meant prioritizing relationship-building over rapid change. By taking time to rebuild trust and involve staff in shaping the school's direction, she created a foundation for sustainable growth. Her vision didn't disappear—it simply evolved to include the voices of her team.

> **Leadership is often a balancing act between your vision and the reality of your school's current state.**

Creating Systems for Transparency, Collaboration, and Accountability

One of the most powerful ways to cultivate organizational awareness is by creating systems that reflect and reinforce the values of your school. These systems serve as the scaffolding that supports transparency, collaboration, and accountability:

Building Transparency Transparency begins with communication. Leaders who openly share their thought processes, decisions, and challenges build trust and reduce uncertainty. Melissa adopted a practice of monthly "state of the school" updates, in which she shared progress on initiatives, acknowledged setbacks, and invited questions. This openness signaled to her staff that she valued their partnership and was committed to honest dialogue.

Fostering Collaboration Collaboration thrives in environments where people feel heard and valued. Melissa established cross-grade teams to tackle school-wide goals, ensuring that every voice—from kindergarten to fifth grade—had a seat at the table. These teams didn't just produce better ideas; they also strengthened relationships across the school, breaking down silos and fostering a sense of shared purpose.

Ensuring Accountability Accountability is not about micromanaging—it's about creating clarity around expectations and follow-through. Melissa introduced a system of shared commitments, where teams set their own goals and regularly reviewed progress together. By involving staff in setting expectations, Melissa created a culture of mutual accountability that was both empowering and effective.

Adaptive Leadership in Action

Cultivating organizational awareness also requires adaptability. No two schools are alike, and the needs of your community will evolve over time. Adaptive leadership is about staying curious, experimenting with new approaches, and being willing to pivot when circumstances change.

When Melissa's district introduced a new initiative focused on social-emotional learning, she recognized both its potential and the hesitation it sparked among her staff. Instead of enforcing immediate compliance, she approached the rollout with flexibility. She invited staff to share their concerns, offered optional professional development sessions, and highlighted small, successful implementations to build confidence. This adaptive approach allowed the initiative to gain traction organically, rooted in the school's unique culture.

Conclusion: Leading with Awareness

Organizational awareness is the bridge between personal leadership growth and collective impact. It is the lens that allows you to see the school not just as a collection of individuals but as a dynamic, interconnected system. By cultivating this awareness, you align your leadership with the true needs of your community, creating a culture where trust, collaboration, and growth thrive.

As you reflect on your own leadership journey, remember that awareness is not a destination—it's a practice. By staying curious, listening deeply, and adapting thoughtfully, you can lead your school with clarity and purpose.

Reflection Prompt

Think about your school's culture. What unspoken norms, values, or dynamics shape its day-to-day operations? How can you deepen your understanding of these factors to better align your leadership with the needs of your school community?

LESSONS LEARNED

As superintendent of Sunset Valley School District, Dr. Kim prided herself on her high emotional intelligence. She knew her strengths and triggers, managed stress well, and communicated clearly with her cabinet. She considered herself a self-aware leader, content that she had "done the work" internally. But lately, she'd sensed unrest in the district, a subtle but growing dissonance between what she thought was happening and how people actually felt. Enrollment patterns were shifting, a new math curriculum rollout had hit unexpected snags, and conversations with building principals felt increasingly cautious and guarded.

One Wednesday morning, after a budget meeting that left her feeling disconnected from the participants, Dr. Kim decided she needed more than personal insight. She recalled the chapter's lessons about organizational awareness—learning to read the culture, spot blind spots, and understand how decisions played out across the system. Was something in the district's culture, beyond her personal interactions, affecting trust and collaboration?

She started simply: instead of relying solely on formal reports and scheduled presentations, Dr. Kim spent a week visiting schools unannounced, not to evaluate, but to observe and listen. At Sunrise Elementary, she noticed that teachers who excelled at collaboration were tucked away in separate wings, rarely crossing paths. At Westview Middle, the principal mentioned offhandedly that the staff often felt blindsided by district-level changes. At Cedar High, student leaders candidly expressed that they wanted more input on academic policies. None of these observations alone were startling, but together they painted a picture of a culture that prized harmony yet avoided difficult conversations. People nodded politely in meetings, then implemented changes half-heartedly or with quiet resentment.

Dr. Kim also examined her communication patterns. Often, district updates were shared through official memos and formal announcements. She realized that while efficient, these methods conveyed decisions without inviting input. Principals, teachers, and even students felt their perspectives arrived too late in the process to influence outcomes. Instead of feeling valued, stakeholders felt like an afterthought.

During a principal roundtable the following week, Dr. Kim tried a different approach. She put aside her prepared notes and said, "I've been hearing that some of our processes feel top-down and rushed. I'd like to understand what that looks like from where you sit." It was a simple invitation, but it opened a floodgate of insights. One principal explained that her teachers were reluctant to embrace the new math curriculum because they'd had no voice in selecting it. Another said that at times, decisions seemed to disregard established traditions that anchored the school community. A third noted that while Dr. Kim personally was approachable, the district's structures didn't invite dialogue early enough.

Instead of defending the existing systems, Dr. Kim listened attentively. She acknowledged these concerns and asked questions: "What would more meaningful involvement look like?" "How can we ensure that feedback reaches decision-makers at the right time?" "In what ways can we honor our traditions while still moving forward?" These inquiries revealed something crucial: the district needed systems that supported transparency, collaboration, and accountability, not just good intentions from leadership.

Armed with this broader understanding, Dr. Kim worked with a small task force of principals, teachers, and even a student representative to redesign the district's decision-making processes. They created "design thinking groups" for major initiatives, bringing stakeholders in early to brainstorm and refine ideas. They developed a feedback loop where pilot programs were tested in one or two schools first, with open forums to gather reactions before district-wide implementation. They also established a tradition of quarterly "district dialogues," informal gatherings where anyone—staff, parents, students, or community members—could raise concerns or offer suggestions.

As these new structures took shape, the climate began to shift. Principals who once approached district mandates cautiously started speaking candidly, knowing their input was welcomed and acted upon. Teachers reported feeling more respected, their experience and expertise no longer sidelined. Students appreciated that their voices mattered, even if they didn't always get what they requested. Over time, decisions felt more aligned with the district's core values and educational mission, not just the directives from above.

Dr. Kim realized that her earlier self-awareness, while valuable, had been incomplete. She needed to understand the culture and context of Sunset Valley's entire educational ecosystem. By zooming out, reading the subtle cues, asking open-ended questions, and creating spaces for honest dialogue, she developed a richer, fuller awareness of the organization she led. No longer was she just the self-aware leader with personal insight; she had become an organizationally aware leader who could navigate complexity, honor diverse perspectives, and foster a culture of trust and shared purpose.

In this way, the lessons from Chapter Thirteen came to life. By looking beyond herself and cultivating organizational awareness, Dr. Kim transformed both her leadership and the district's overall climate, ensuring that everyone felt seen, heard, and part of the journey forward.

CHAPTER FOURTEEN

The Legacy of a Self-Aware Leader: Building a Culture of Continuous Improvement

S elf-awareness is one of the most powerful traits a leader can possess. It shapes how leaders see themselves, how they interact with others, and how they navigate challenges. Leaders who are aware of their strengths and limitations create an atmosphere of authenticity, trust, and openness. Their self-awareness allows them to model continuous improvement, inspiring others to do the same. This chapter will explore how self-aware leaders can build a culture of growth that encourages everyone in an organization to strive for excellence, embrace learning, and cultivate resilience.

When a leader is self-aware, they understand that they don't have all the answers—and they're comfortable with that. Instead of relying solely on their expertise, they actively seek input from others, acknowledge their limitations, and embrace vulnerability. This approach fosters a safe space where team members feel valued, empowered, and motivated to grow. As we delve into the impact of self-aware leadership, we'll explore how these leaders cultivate a culture in which continuous improvement is the norm, and personal development is encouraged at every level.

The Power of Self-Awareness in Leadership

> When a leader is self-aware, they understand that they don't have all the answers—and they're comfortable with that.

Self-awareness enables leaders to operate with a deep understanding of who they are, how they're perceived, and the impact they have on others. Leaders who possess this awareness can make more intentional decisions, communicate effectively, and foster an environment that values growth and learning. Here's why self-awareness is essential in creating a culture of continuous improvement:

1. **Modeling Authenticity and Vulnerability**
Self-aware leaders understand their limitations and aren't afraid to acknowledge them. This openness builds trust and sets the tone for an honest, growth-focused environment. When leaders are willing to admit their own challenges or ask for help, it sends a powerful message to the team: growth comes from honesty, humility, and a willingness to learn.

2. **Encouraging Open Dialogue and Feedback**
Self-aware leaders value feedback, recognizing it as an opportunity for growth. By inviting feedback from their teams, they create a feedback-rich environment where people feel safe sharing their ideas and perspectives. This culture of open dialogue empowers team members to learn from each other, fosters mutual respect, and fuels continuous improvement.

3. **Setting Realistic Goals and Expectations**

Leaders who are self-aware set realistic goals that are aligned with both their strengths and their areas for development. By recognizing their limitations, they avoid overcommitting and make room for others to step in and contribute. This approach not only fosters a balanced, sustainable work environment but also encourages team members to stretch their capabilities.

4. **Building Stronger Relationships and Trust**

Self-awareness allows leaders to understand the emotional impact they have on others. They are attuned to their team's needs and respond empathetically, building strong relationships grounded in trust. By being genuinely invested in their team's growth and well-being, self-aware leaders create a supportive, collaborative environment that strengthens loyalty and commitment.

5. **Creating a Learning-Oriented Mindset**

Self-aware leaders know that they don't have all the answers and are eager to learn. This mindset encourages curiosity and innovation, as team members are inspired to adopt the same approach. In a culture that values learning, people are more willing to take risks, try new ideas, and challenge the status quo—all essential components of continuous improvement.

How Self-Awareness Inspires a Culture of Continuous Improvement

A self-aware leader inspires continuous improvement by modeling growth, creating safe spaces for development, and establishing practices that encourage learning and reflection. Here's how self-awareness can fuel an environment where everyone is motivated to grow:

1. **Leading by Example**

   One of the most effective ways to inspire growth in others is to model it yourself. Self-aware leaders are committed to their own development, whether through seeking feedback, learning new skills, or reflecting on their actions. By demonstrating a growth mindset, they show their team that improvement is a lifelong journey, and that setbacks or challenges are steppingstones toward excellence.

   For example, a self-aware leader might openly discuss a professional development course they're taking or share insights from a recent mistake. This openness normalizes growth and encourages others to pursue their own learning journeys.

2. **Promoting Psychological Safety**

   A culture of growth requires a safe space for people to make mistakes, ask questions, and seek support. Self-aware leaders recognize the importance of psychological safety and are intentional about creating an environment where team members feel valued and respected. By responding calmly to challenges, acknowledging their own vulnerabilities, and celebrating both successes and learning experiences, they build a foundation of trust.

   For instance, when a team member admits a mistake, a self-aware leader might say, "Thank you for bringing this up. Let's discuss how we can learn from it." This response reassures the team member that they're in a supportive environment where their development matters.

3. **Inviting Feedback Regularly**

   Self-aware leaders don't wait for formal reviews to gather feedback; they seek it regularly and use it as a tool for continuous improvement. By asking for input on their leadership style, decisions, and team dynamics, they signal that growth is an ongoing priority. When team members see their leader embracing feedback, they become more comfortable offering and receiving it themselves.

For example, a self-aware leader might implement a regular "pulse check" where team members can share their thoughts on what's working well and what could improve. This ongoing feedback loop keeps growth top of mind and ensures the team feels heard.

4. Establishing Development Goals for the Team

In a culture of growth, everyone is encouraged to set and pursue personal development goals. Self-aware leaders work with their team members to identify areas for improvement and provide the resources and support to help them succeed. These goals create a sense of purpose and direction, and they ensure that everyone is actively contributing to their own and the team's development.

For instance, a self-aware leader might hold regular one-on-one meetings focused on personal and professional growth, discussing each team member's goals, progress, and potential challenges. This focus on individual growth shows a commitment to continuous improvement on a team-wide scale.

5. Encouraging Reflection and Learning from Experience

Self-aware leaders understand the power of reflection in personal and professional growth. By encouraging teams to reflect on their experiences, both positive and negative, they help them learn from the past and make better decisions in the future. This habit of reflection cultivates a culture where people are thoughtful, mindful, and open to self-improvement.

For example, after completing a major project, a self-aware leader might organize a debriefing session where the team reflects on what went well and what could be improved. This reflective practice reinforces the value of continuous learning and growth.

6. Celebrating Growth as Much as Achievement

In a culture of growth, progress is celebrated just as much as success. Self-aware leaders recognize that growth isn't always linear, and they make an effort to acknowledge each team member's development, even if the end goals haven't been fully achieved. By celebrating growth, they reinforce the idea that improvement is valuable in itself.

A self-aware leader might celebrate a team member who took on a challenging task for the first time, acknowledging the courage and effort rather than just the outcome. This recognition fosters a sense of pride and encourages others to embrace new challenges.

7. Encouraging Cross-Functional Learning and Mentorship

Self-aware leaders understand that growth often happens when people step out of their comfort zones and learn from others. They encourage cross-functional learning and mentorship opportunities that expose team members to new skills, perspectives, and ideas. This approach not only enriches individual growth but also strengthens collaboration across the organization.

For example, a self-aware leader might set up mentorship pairings where experienced team members work with newer ones to share insights and skills. This exchange fosters a culture where everyone learns from each other and values shared knowledge.

Building a Legacy of Growth

The impact of a self-aware leader goes far beyond their time with a team. By cultivating a culture of growth, they create a legacy that endures, influencing how people think, learn, and develop long after they've moved on. This legacy of growth empowers individuals to continuously improve, embrace challenges, and seek excellence.

Self-aware leaders recognize that their role is to inspire others to reach their full potential. They invest in people, nurture talent, and create an environment where everyone feels capable of contributing and evolving. The ripple effects of this approach can transform an organization, creating a culture that values learning, curiosity, and resilience.

Conclusion: The Enduring Impact of Self-Aware Leadership

The journey to self-awareness is ongoing, requiring reflection, humility, and a commitment to growth. As a self-aware leader, you have the opportunity to inspire those around you, not through perfection, but through authenticity, openness, and an unwavering dedication to learning. By leading with self-awareness, you build trust, foster resilience, and create a culture where everyone is encouraged to improve continuously.

The legacy of a self-aware leader is profound. It's a legacy that shapes the culture of an organization, encouraging people to embrace growth, seek feedback, and strive for excellence. When leaders are self-aware, they create a workplace where every individual feels valued, motivated, and empowered to make meaningful contributions. This legacy doesn't just end with one leader; it becomes woven into the organization's DNA, inspiring future leaders to continue fostering a culture of growth.

Reflection Prompt

Think about a time in your leadership journey when you avoided addressing a difficult emotion—whether it was frustration, fear, self-doubt, or feeling overwhelmed. How did that avoidance impact your well-being, your decision-making, or your relationships with others?

Looking back, what valuable insight might that emotion have been trying to reveal to you? Now, consider a current challenge you are facing as a leader. What emotions are present beneath the surface? How might leaning into those feelings—rather than pushing them aside—help you make a clearer, more thoughtful decision or strengthen trust with your team?

Journal your thoughts, focusing on this question:

How can I begin to see my emotions not as obstacles, but as essential signals guiding me toward healthier, more authentic leadership?

LESSONS LEARNED

When Dr. Hughes first became principal of Willowbrook High School, the campus was known for its stability—routine procedures, decent test scores, and a staff that stuck to familiar methods. But there was also a hidden cost to that comfort: innovation was limited, professional growth felt optional, and reflection was rare. Willowbrook wasn't failing, but it was coasting.

Dr. Hughes had read extensively about self-awareness and continuous improvement before taking the role. She understood that genuine progress required ongoing, honest reflection—not just for her, but for everyone on campus. She arrived determined to lead by example, openly acknowledging her own learning curve and inviting others to join her in the journey.

In her first year, Dr. Hughes introduced a simple practice: regular "growth conversations" during staff meetings. Teachers were encouraged to share not only successes but also the lessons they learned from setbacks. She began by modeling this herself. After a particularly chaotic rollout of a new attendance system, she admitted, "I realized I didn't gather enough input from our front office team before making changes, and that led to confusion. Next time, I'll make sure to listen more carefully before acting." Instead of defensive justifications, she focused on what she learned.

Staff members were initially hesitant—fearful that talking about mistakes would lower their standing or invite blame. But as weeks passed, Dr. Hughes's consistent humility and curiosity reassured them. Over time, teachers started volunteering their own reflections: a math teacher admitting that her new group-work strategy needed refinement, a counselor describing how a failed assembly plan taught her about scheduling conflicts, a department chair openly wondering how to better integrate technology without overwhelming colleagues.

As trust deepened, Dr. Hughes worked with teacher leaders to establish Professional Learning Communities (PLCs) where instructional data, student feedback, and peer observations fed into a cycle of improvement. The question at the heart of these PLCs was always, "How can we do better for our students?" No one pointed fingers if a new approach didn't yield immediate results. Instead, they asked, "What can we try next?" Continuous improvement became the norm—not just an initiative but a mindset.

Parents and students noticed the shift, too. The parent advisory council found that their suggestions were met not with polite nods, but with genuine curiosity. Students who once felt like passive recipients of instruction began participating in feedback sessions about school climate and course offerings. Dr. Hughes modeled this responsiveness by holding student forums each semester and publicly sharing what she'd learned and what actions would follow. Even board members praised Willowbrook's culture, using it as a model for other schools in the district.

Eight years later, when Dr. Hughes announced her plans to retire, some worried that the spirit of continual reflection and learning would fade without her. But by then, the habit of inquiry and improvement was woven into the school's fabric. The staff didn't rely on Dr. Hughes alone to prompt growth discussions—they had PLCs, peer coaching teams, and "lesson study" groups that persisted on their own. New teachers, upon joining Willowbrook, were mentored not just in curriculum and routines, but in the art of self-reflection and collaborative improvement.

On Dr. Hughes's final day, the faculty gathered in the library. A veteran teacher, one who had once resisted changing her methods, stood up to toast the outgoing principal. "We used to say, 'If it ain't broke, don't fix it.' But you showed us that we could be good and still strive to be better. You didn't just give us new strategies; you helped us embrace growth as a constant process. Even without you here, we'll keep asking questions, learning from each other, and moving forward."

Dr. Hughes smiled, proud but also humbled. Her legacy wasn't about her personal achievements or grand innovations. It was the lasting culture she and her staff had built together—a place where self-awareness and continuous improvement were second nature, fueling the school's progress long after she handed over the keys to her successor.

In this way, the lessons from Chapter Fourteen came to life. By continually cultivating her own self-awareness and modeling reflective growth, Dr. Hughes created a community that didn't stand still once good was "good enough." Instead, Willowbrook High continued to evolve, learn, and innovate, ensuring that the legacy of self-awareness and continuous improvement would endure for generations to come.

FINAL THOUGHTS

The Path of the Self-Aware Leader

Imagine you're on a journey—one that's more winding than straight, more challenging than easy, and more fulfilling than you ever anticipated. This is the journey of self-aware leadership. You set off with excitement, equipped with maps, tools, and stories from leaders who came before you. Yet, as you travel deeper, you realize that to be a truly effective leader, to inspire others, and to leave a lasting impact, you must go beyond knowing what makes you strong. You must also come to terms with what makes you human. You need to know your strengths and your weaknesses, and this understanding will reveal the deeper dimensions of leadership and self-awareness.

Let's take a look back over the road you've traveled in this book, revisiting some of the most pivotal stops along the way. Through stories, insights, and practices, this journey has pushed you to explore self-awareness at its fullest—embracing not only your skills but also your imperfections. Together, we've uncovered how these two facets, when understood and aligned, help create a leader capable of empowering others, inspiring growth, and building lasting change.

The Leader You're Not: Facing Your Blind Spots

The journey began with a powerful realization: that self-awareness isn't just about knowing your strengths; it's about recognizing what you don't see. In leadership, as in life, we each have blind spots. These are areas where our strengths fade into shadows, and weaknesses silently take the stage. These blind spots, if left unchecked, can silently sabotage relationships, trust, and performance.

Yet, rather than seeing these blind spots as flaws to hide, this book encouraged you to approach them with curiosity. Self-aware leaders are those who dare to explore their blind spots and ask questions like, What don't I know about myself that others see? How might my actions impact others in ways I haven't noticed? By embracing your blind spots, you open doors to growth, humility, and a more honest connection with your team. True self-awareness means understanding your limits and seeking feedback from others to help you see beyond what's familiar.

Humble Confidence: The Paradox of Strength and Vulnerability

As you moved deeper into the journey, you discovered the power of "humble confidence"—the delicate dance between strength and vulnerability. Leadership isn't about being invincible; it's about balancing your own self-assuredness with the willingness to admit when you don't have the answers. Leaders who embody humble confidence understand that admitting weakness doesn't diminish their authority—it enhances it.

This lesson challenged the conventional notion that leaders must project unwavering certainty. Instead, it revealed that leadership is strengthened by the courage to ask for help, to invite others into the decision-making process, and to listen. When leaders show their teams that vulnerability is acceptable, they foster a culture where honesty, innovation, and trust can thrive.

The Cost of Perfectionism: Letting Go to Lead Freely

Along the way, you encountered the seductive pull of perfectionism, a habit that so often plagues high-achieving leaders. It's easy to think that perfectionism is a virtue, that it reflects high standards and dedication. But in truth, perfectionism can trap leaders in a cycle of fear, making them reluctant to take risks, delegate, or admit mistakes.

In this chapter, you learned that perfectionism is the silent saboteur that erodes resilience, stifles creativity, and damages morale. The way forward? Embrace a mindset that values progress over perfection. Leaders who let go of the need to be flawless free themselves to experiment, make mistakes, and learn. They inspire their teams to do the same, creating a more adaptable, empowered, and resilient environment.

Listening to Criticism: Turning Weakness into Growth

If there's one skill every self-aware leader needs, it's the ability to listen to feedback—especially when it's uncomfortable. Receiving criticism can be challenging, yet it's an essential ingredient in the recipe for growth. Self-aware leaders view feedback not as a judgment but as a tool for understanding where they can improve.

In this part of the journey, you learned how to welcome feedback with curiosity rather than defensiveness, seeing it as a gift that reveals blind spots and encourages growth. Leaders who actively seek feedback create a culture where everyone feels empowered to learn, speak openly, and improve together. By embracing criticism, leaders model humility and inspire their teams to adopt a growth mindset.

Delegate, Don't Dominate: The Art of Empowering Others

A vital lesson in self-awareness is recognizing when you're holding on too tightly. Leaders who are self-aware know their limits and understand that they can't—and shouldn't—do it all. They realize that delegation isn't just about lightening their own load; it's about empowering others, developing talent, and building a collaborative, high-performing team.

This chapter emphasized the value of trust, the importance of empowering team members, and the growth that happens when leaders step back to let others lead. By letting go, self-aware leaders foster autonomy and confidence in their teams, creating an environment where everyone is encouraged to contribute their best.

Managing Emotions: Leading with Composure Under Pressure

Leadership is filled with high-stakes moments that test resilience, patience, and composure. In this chapter, you delved into emotional regulation and the importance of staying grounded, especially in challenging situations. Self-aware leaders understand the power of their emotional impact; they know that how they handle stress influences the entire team's morale and performance.

By learning to manage your emotions and model calmness under pressure, you reinforce an atmosphere of stability and trust. Emotions are an inevitable part of leadership, but self-aware leaders know how to channel them constructively, turning even the most challenging situations into opportunities for growth.

The Silent Saboteurs: Addressing Insecurity and Self-Doubt

Every leader, no matter how experienced, has moments of insecurity and self-doubt. But self-aware leaders recognize that these silent saboteurs can subtly undermine their effectiveness if left unchecked. The journey through this chapter taught you how to confront these internal doubts, not by ignoring them, but by examining their origins and reframing them.

Self-aware leaders develop the resilience to face their insecurities, understanding that vulnerability doesn't make them weak. In fact, it helps them connect more authentically with others, model resilience, and show that growth is a continuous journey.

Visible Leadership: Leading with Authenticity in the Face of Adversity

As you ventured deeper into self-awareness, you encountered the concept of transparency in leadership—acknowledging limitations and being open about challenges. Self-aware leaders understand that honesty fosters trust, and they're not afraid to lead with authenticity, even when it means revealing their struggles. This level of transparency creates a culture where people feel safe to express themselves and take risks.

By sharing their own challenges, self-aware leaders set a powerful example, showing their teams that it's okay to be human. This authenticity strengthens relationships, inspires loyalty, and fosters a team culture rooted in mutual respect and growth.

Adapt or Falter: Knowing When to Change Your Approach

Leadership isn't static; it requires adaptability. The self-aware leader is flexible, ready to adjust their approach to meet the needs of a constantly changing environment. This chapter taught you to recognize when a shift is needed, whether due to team dynamics, project demands, or personal growth.

Adaptable leaders are resilient, embracing change and navigating uncertainty with an open mind. By understanding when and how to adapt, self-aware leaders ensure they remain effective, connected, and responsive to the evolving needs of their teams and organizations.

The Legacy of a Self-Aware Leader: Building a Culture of Continuous Improvement

At the end of the journey, you come to realize the true legacy of self-aware leadership: a culture of continuous growth. Leaders who embrace their strengths and weaknesses, who learn from feedback, who empower others, and who foster open dialogue create a legacy that goes beyond their tenure. They leave behind a team that values growth, embraces learning, and strives for excellence.

Self-aware leaders inspire others to embark on their own journeys of growth, building a workplace culture in which everyone is encouraged to reach their full potential. This culture of growth doesn't merely benefit the team; it shapes the organization's future, creating a foundation for resilience, adaptability, and success.

A Final Reflection

As you stand at the end of this journey, looking back on the lessons you've learned, consider the leader you've become. You've navigated through self-awareness, embraced your strengths and weaknesses, and learned how to build a culture that values growth and improvement. The journey of self-aware leadership is continuous—each experience, each challenge, and each moment of reflection brings you closer to becoming the leader you aspire to be.

Reflect on the legacy you want to leave as a leader. What impact do you hope to have on those you lead, and what steps can you take today to build a culture of continuous improvement?

Now…go and make it happen!

Recommended Reading

Brown, B. (2018). *Dare to Lead: Brave Work. Tough Conversations. Whole Hearts*. New York, NY: Random House. Brown's work on vulnerability and courage in leadership highlights the value of authenticity and transparency in building resilient teams and a culture of trust.

Collins, J. (2001). *Good to Great: Why Some Companies Make the Leap… and Others Don't*. New York, NY: Harper Business. This classic text on business and leadership delves into the qualities that drive companies to success, emphasizing disciplined thought, action, and the importance of the "Level 5 Leader."

Covey, S. R. (1989). *The 7 Habits of Highly Effective People: Powerful Lessons in Personal Change*. New York, NY: Free Press. Covey's foundational work on personal effectiveness outlines habits that promote self-awareness, resilience, and purposeful leadership.

Dweck, C. S. (2006). *Mindset: The New Psychology of Success*. New York, NY: Random House. Dweck's research on growth versus fixed mindsets provides insights into how leaders can foster a culture of continuous improvement and adaptability.

Goleman, D. (1995). *Emotional Intelligence: Why It Can Matter More Than IQ*. New York, NY: Bantam Books. Goleman's pioneering work on emotional intelligence underscores the role of self-awareness, empathy, and emotional regulation in effective leadership.

Heifetz, R. A., & Linsky, M. (2002). *Leadership on the Line: Staying Alive Through the Dangers of Leading*. Boston, MA: Harvard Business Review Press. This work explores the challenges and risks of adaptive leadership, offering strategies for resilience and the courage to lead authentically.

Kegan, R., & Lahey, L. L. (2009). *Immunity to Change: How to Overcome It and Unlock the Potential in Yourself and Your Organization*. Boston, MA: Harvard Business Review Press. Kegan and Lahey delve into self-awareness and personal growth, addressing the psychological barriers that can hinder leaders and organizations from achieving transformative change.

Lencioni, P. (2002). *The Five Dysfunctions of a Team: A Leadership Fable*. San Francisco, CA: Jossey-Bass. Lencioni's work focuses on building cohesive teams through trust, accountability, and commitment, laying a foundation for leaders to foster a growth-oriented culture.

Schein, E. H. (2010). *Organizational Culture and Leadership*. San Francisco, CA: Jossey-Bass. Schein's comprehensive study of organizational culture offers insights into how leaders shape and reinforce values, norms, and behaviors within their teams and organizations.

Scazzero, P. (2015). *The Emotionally Healthy Leader: How Transforming Your Inner Life Will Deeply Transform Your Church, Team, and the World*. Grand Rapids, MI: Zondervan. Scazzero's work on emotional health in leadership provides guidance on self-awareness, humility, and creating a workplace that values well-being and authenticity.

Senge, P. M. (1990). *The Fifth Discipline: The Art and Practice of the Learning Organization*. New York, NY: Doubleday. Senge's work introduces the concept of the "learning organization," emphasizing systems thinking and continuous improvement as essential for sustainable success.

Simon, S. (2017). *Leaders Eat Last: Why Some Teams Pull Together and Others Don't*. New York, NY: Portfolio. Sinek explores how leaders create a culture of safety and trust, which promotes growth, resilience, and unity within teams.

Wheatley, M. J. (2006). *Leadership and the New Science: Discovering Order in a Chaotic World*. San Francisco, CA: Berrett-Koehler Publishers. Wheatley's book explores leadership in complex, rapidly changing environments, offering insights into adaptability and the importance of a learning culture.

About the Author

Scott Borba is a seasoned leader, educator, and advocate for personal growth and self-awareness in the world of public education. Recognized as a 2017 National Distinguished Principal with the National Association of Elementary School Principals (NAESP) and 2021 Superintendent/Principal of the Year with the Association of California School Administrators (ACSA), Scott has earned a reputation for excellence and dedication in his field. With over two decades of experience in leadership roles, including twelve years as a professor of school law at CSU Stanislaus, Scott has dedicated his career to creating environments where both students and educators feel empowered to grow, innovate, and succeed. As Superintendent and Principal of Le Grand Union Elementary School District, Scott combines his passion for education with a commitment to fostering leadership that is honest, adaptable, and growth-oriented.

Driven by the belief that true leadership requires both confidence and humility, Scott has developed a unique approach that emphasizes the importance of knowing one's strengths as well as embracing one's limitations. His work is rooted in the idea that leaders who are self-aware and open about their own growth inspire others to do the same, ultimately building a culture of continuous improvement. Scott is known for his engaging, down-to-earth style, connecting with readers and colleagues through stories that are as insightful as they are relatable.

Outside of his work in education, Scott is a dedicated family man, avid reader, and lifelong learner who values time with his family and community. His dedication to guiding the next generation of leaders extends beyond the workplace, as he actively mentors aspiring leaders and supports initiatives that cultivate emotional health, resilience, and empathy. Connect with Scott on X at @LgeSupt or on LinkedIn.

More from ConnectEDD Publishing

Since 2015, ConnectEDD has worked to transform education by empowering educators to become better-equipped to teach, learn, and lead. What started as a small company designed to provide professional learning events for educators has grown to include a variety of services to help educators and administrators address essential challenges. ConnectEDD offers instructional and leadership coaching, professional development workshops focusing on a variety of educational topics, a roster of nationally recognized educator associates who possess hands-on knowledge and experience, educational conferences custom-designed to meet the specific needs of schools, districts, and state/national organizations, and ongoing, personalized support, both virtually and onsite. In 2020, ConnectEDD expanded to include publishing services designed to provide busy educators with books and resources consisting of practical information on a wide variety of teaching, learning, and leadership topics. Please visit us online at connecteddpublishing.com or contact us at: info@connecteddpublishing.com

Recent Publications:

Live Your Excellence: Action Guide by Jimmy Casas

Culturize: Action Guide by Jimmy Casas

Daily Inspiration for Educators: Positive Thoughts for Every Day of the Year by Jimmy Casas

Eyes on Culture: Multiply Excellence in Your School by Emily Paschall

Pause. Breathe. Flourish. Living Your Best Life as an Educator by William D. Parker

L.E.A.R.N.E.R. Finding the True, Good, and Beautiful in Education by Marita Diffenbaugh

Educator Reflection Tips Volume II: Refining Our Practice by Jami Fowler-White

Handle With Care: Managing Difficult Situations in Schools with Dignity and Respect by Jimmy Casas and Joy Kelly

Disruptive Thinking: Preparing Learners for Their Future by Eric Sheninger

Permission to be Great: Increasing Engagement in Your School by Dan Butler

Daily Inspiration for Educators: Positive Thoughts for Every Day of the Year, Volume II by Jimmy Casas

The 6 Literacy Levers: Creating a Community of Readers by Brad Gustafson

The Educator's ATLAS: Your Roadmap to Engagement by Weston Kieschnick

MORE FROM CONNECTEDD PUBLISHING

In This Season: Words for the Heart by Todd Nesloney, LaNesha Tabb, Tanner Olson, and Alice Lee

Leading with a Humble Heart: A 40-Day Devotional for Leaders by Zac Bauermaster

Recalibrate the Culture: Our Why…Our Work…Our Values by Jimmy Casas

Creating Curious Classrooms: The Beauty of Questions by Emma Chiappetta

Crafting the Culture: 45 Reflections on What Matters Most by Joe Sanfelippo and Jeffrey Zoul

Improving School Mental Health: The Thriving School Community Solution by Charle Peck and Dr. Cameron Caswell

Building Authenticity: A Blueprint for the Leader Inside You by Todd Nesloney and Tyler Cook

Connecting Through Conversation: A Playbook for Talking with Kids by Erika Bare and Tiffany Burns

The Dream Factory: Designing a Purposeful Life by Mark Trumbo

Stories Behind Stances: Creating Empathy Through Hearing "The Other Side" by Chris Singleton

Happy Eyes: Becoming All Things to All People by Ryan Tillman

The Generative Age Artificial Intelligence and the Future of Education by Alana Winnick

Recalibrate the Culture: Action Guide by Jimmy Casas

Leading with PEOPLE: A Six Pillar Framework for Fruitful Leadership by Zac Bauermaster

A School Leader's Guide to Reclaiming Purpose by Frederick C. Buskey

Foundations of an Elite Culture: Building Success with High Standards and a Positive Environment by David Arencibia

Personalize: Meeting the Needs of All Learners by Eric Sheninger and Nicki Slaugh

The Five Principles of Educator Professionalism: Rebuilding Trust in Schools by Nason Lollar

Words on the Wall: Culturizing Your Classroom For Observable Impact by Jimmy Casas and Cale Birk

School of Engagement: 45 Activities to Ignite Student Learning by Jonathan Alsheimer

Intentional Instructional Moves: Strategic Steps to Accelerate Student Learning by Sherry St. Clair

Overcoming Education: Complex Challenges, Difficult People, and the Art of Making a Difference by Brad R. Gustafson

The Language of Behavior: A Framework to Elevate Student Success by Charle Peck and Joshua Stamper

Whose Permission Are You Waiting For? An Educator's Guide to Doing What You Love by William D. Parker

www.ingramcontent.com/pod-product-compliance
Lightning Source LLC
Chambersburg PA
CBHW060950050426
42337CB00053B/3871